Dedication

Moaz Safi Yousef al-Kasasbeh
May 29, 1988–January 3, 2015

Also by Yatir Nitzany

Conversational Portuguese Quick and Easy

....

Conversational Spanish Quick and Easy

....

Conversational Italian Quick and Easy

....

Conversational French Quick and Easy

....

Conversational German Quick and Easy

....

Conversational Russian Quick and Easy

....

Conversational Polish Quick and Easy

....

Conversational Hebrew Quick and Easy

....

Conversational Yiddish Quick and Easy

....

Conversational Arabic Quick and Easy
Classical Arabic

....

Conversational Arabic Quick and Easy
Palestinian Dialect

....

Conversational Arabic Quick and Easy
Egyptian Dialect

....

Conversational Arabic Quick and Easy
Jordanian Dialect

....

Conversational Arabic Quick and Easy
Emirati Dialect

....

Conversational Arabic Quick and Easy
Iraqi Arabic

Conversational Arabic Quick and Easy

LEVANTINE SERIES

YATIR NITZANY

Foreword

About Myself

For many years I struggled to learn Spanish, and I still knew no more than about twenty words. Consequently, I was extremely frustrated. One day I stumbled upon this method as I was playing around with word combinations. Suddenly, I came to the realization that every language has a certain core group of words that are most commonly used and, simply by learning them, one could gain the ability to engage in quick and easy conversational Spanish.

I discovered which words those were, and I narrowed them down to three hundred and fifty that, once memorized, one could connect and create one's own sentences. The variations were and are infinite! By using this incredibly simple technique, I could converse at a proficient level and speak Spanish. Within a week, I astonished my Spanish-speaking friends with my newfound ability. The next semester I registered at my university for a Spanish language course, and I applied the same principles I had learned in that class (grammar, additional vocabulary, future and past tense, etc.) to those three hundred and fifty words I already had memorized, and immediately I felt as if I had grown wings and learned how to fly.

At the end of the semester, we took a class trip to San José, Costa Rica. I was like a fish in water, while the rest of my classmates were floundering and still struggling to converse. Throughout the following months, I again applied the same principle to other languages—French, Portuguese, Italian, and Arabic, all of which I now speak proficiently, thanks to this very simple technique.

This method is by far the fastest way to master quick and easy conversational language skills. There is no other technique that compares to my concept. It is effective, it worked for me, and it will work for you. Be consistent with my program, and you too will succeed the way I and many, many others have.

Contents

Introduction to the Program. 8

Memorization Made Easy 11

The Lebanese Dialect 12

The Palestinian Dialect. 42

The Syrian Dialect. 75

The Jordanian Dialect. 109

Conclusion 143

INTRODUCTION TO
THE PROGRAM

People often dream about learning a foreign language, but usually they never do it. Some feel that they just won't be able to do it while others believe that they don't have the time. Whatever your reason is, it's time to set that aside. With my new method, you will have enough time, and you will not fail. You will actually learn how to speak the fundamentals of the language—fluently in as little as a few days. Of course, you won't speak perfect Arabic at first, but you will certainly gain significant proficiency. For example, if you travel to Lebanon or Syria, the Palestinian Territories, or the Hashemite Kingdom of Jordan, you will almost effortlessly be able engage in basic conversational communication with the locals in the present tense and you will no longer be intimidated by culture shock. It's time to relax. Learning a language is a valuable skill that connects people of multiple cultures around the world—and you now have the tools to join them.

How does my method work? I have taken twenty-seven of the most commonly used languages in the world and distilled from them the three hundred and fifty most frequently used words in any language. This process took three years of observation and research, and during that time, I determined which words I felt were most important for this method of basic conversational communication. In that time, I chose these words in such a way that they were structurally interrelated and that, when combined, form sentences. Thus, once you succeed in memorizing these words, you will be able to combine these words and form your own sentences. The words are spread over twenty pages. In fact, there are just nine basic words that will effectively build bridges, enabling you to speak in an understandable manner (please see Building Bridges at the end of each section). The words will also combine easily in sentences, for example, enabling you to ask simple questions, make basic statements, and obtain a rudimentary understanding of others' communications. I have also created Memorization Made Easy techniques for this program in order to help with the memorization of the vocabulary. Please see Reading and Pronunciation of Arabic accents in order to gain proficiency in the reading and pronunciation of the Arabic language prior to starting this program.

My book is mainly intended for basic present tense vocal communication, meaning anyone can easily use it to "get by" linguistically while visiting a foreign country without learning the entire language. With practice, you will be 100 percent understandable to native speakers, which is your aim. One disclaimer: this is not a grammar book, though it does address minute and essential grammar rules. Therefore, understanding complex sentences with obscure words in Arabic is beyond the scope of this book.

People who have tried this method have been successful, and by the time you finish this book, you will understand and be understood in basic conversational Arabic. This is the best basis to learn not only the Arabic language but any language. This is an entirely revolutionary, no-fail concept, and your ability to combine the pieces of the "language puzzle" together will come with great ease, especially if you use this program prior to beginning an Arabic class.

This is the best program that was ever designed to teach the reader how to become conversational. Other conversational programs will only teach you phrases. But this is the only program that will teach you how to create your own sentences for the purpose of becoming conversational.

MEMORIZATION MADE EASY

There is no doubt the three hundred and fifty words in my program are the required essentials in order to engage in quick and easy basic conversation in any foreign language. However, some people may experience difficulty in the memorization. For this reason, I created Memorization Made Easy. This memorization technique will make this program so simple and fun that it's unbelievable! I have spread the words over the following twenty pages. Each page contains a vocabulary table of ten to fifteen words. Below every vocabulary box, sentences are composed from the words on the page that you have just studied. This aids greatly in memorization. Once you succeed in memorizing the first page, then proceed to the second page. Upon completion of the second page, go back to the first and review. Then proceed to the third page. After memorizing the third, go back to the first and second and repeat. And so on. As you continue, begin to combine words and create your own sentences in your head. Every time you proceed to the following page, you will notice words from the previous pages will be present in those simple sentences as well, because repetition is one of the most crucial aspects in learning any foreign language. Upon completion of your twenty pages, congratulations, you have absorbed the required words and gained a basic, quick-and-easy proficiency and you should now be able to create your own sentences and say anything you wish in the Arabic language. This is a crash course in conversational Arabic, and it works!

Conversational Arabic Quick and Easy

LEBANESE DIALECT

YATIR NITZANY

THE LEBANESE ARABIC DIALECT

Lebanese Arabic is a Levantine dialect. The term "Levantine" derives from "Levant," which is the geographical region of the eastern Mediterranean that encompasses Cyprus, Lebanon, Syria, Israel, Palestine, Jordan, and the Hatay Province of southern Turkey. Several languages are spoken in the Levant, one of which is Lebanese Arabic. Lebanese Arabic descends from the traditional Arabic language, though there are many variables that affected the development of the language. Most Lebanese people speak the language, and Arabic remains its written form, despite past attempts by some to make an alphabet system using Latin letters. Some people view Lebanese as merely a dialect of Arabic, while others accept the language as unique. Either way, the word connotations vary in both languages, as do their syntax and vocabularies. Lebanese Arabic uses a bit of Turkish and Aramaic vocabulary and a little French. In general keep in mind that Lebanese Arabic is not an official language but, rather, a colloquial dialect.

Spoken in: Lebanon

ARABIC PRONUNCIATIONS

PLEASE MASTER THE FOLLOWING PAGE IN ARABIC PRONUNCIATIONS PRIOR TO STARTING THE PROGRAM

Kha. For Middle Eastern languages including Arabic, Hebrew, Farsi, Pashto, Urdu, Hindi, etc., and also German, to properly pronounce the kh or ch is essential, for example, *Khaled* (a Muslim name) or *Chanukah* (a Jewish holiday) or *Nacht* ("night" in German). The best way to describe kh or ch is to say "ka" or "ha" while at the same time putting your tongue at the back of your throat and blowing air. It's pronounced similarly to the sound that you make when clearing your throat. Please remember this whenever you come across any word containing a kh in this program.

Ghayin. The Arabic gh is equivalent to the "g" in English, but its pronunciation more closely resembles the French "r," rather than "g." Pronounce it at the back of your throat. The sound is equivalent to what you would make when gargling water. Gha is pronounced more as "rha," rather than as "ga." *Ghada* is pronounced as "rhada." In this program, the symbol for *ghayin* is gh, so keep your eyes peeled.

Aayin is pronounced as a'a, pronounced deep at the back of your throat. Rather similar to the sound one would make when gagging. In the program, the symbol for *aayin* is *a'a, u'u, o'o,* or *i'i.*

Ha is pronounced as "ha." Pronunciation takes place deep at the back of your throat, and for correct pronunciation, one must constrict the back of the throat and exhale air while simultaneously saying "ha." In the program, this strong h ("ha") is emphasized whenever *ha, ah, hi, he,* or *hu* is encountered.

NOTE TO THE READER

The purpose of this book is merely to enable you to communicate in the Lebanese Arabic Dialect. In the program itself (pages 17-38) you may notice that the composition of some of those sentences might sound rather clumsy. This is intentional. These sentences were formulated in a specific way to serve two purposes: to facilitate the easy memorization of the vocabulary and to teach you how to combine the words in order to form your own sentences for quick and easy communication, rather than making complete literal sense in the English language. So keep in mind that this is not a phrase book!

As the title suggests, the sole purpose of this program is for conversational use only. It is based on the mirror translation technique. These sentences, as well as the translations are not incorrect, just a little clumsy. Latin languages, Semitic languages, and Anglo-Germanic languages, as well as a few others, are compatible with the mirror translation technique.

Many users say that this method surpasses any other known language learning technique that is currently out there on the market. Just stick with the program and you will achieve wonders!

Again, I wish to stress this program is by no means, shape, or form a phrase book! The sole purpose of this book is to give you a fundamental platform to enable you to connect certain words to become conversational. Please also read the "Introduction" and the "About Me" section prior to commencing the program.

In order to succeed with my method, please start on the very first page of the program and fully master one page at a time prior to proceeding to the next. Otherwise, you will overwhelm yourself and fail. Please do not skip pages, nor start from the middle of the book.

It is a myth that certain people are born with the talent to learn a language, and this book disproves that myth. With this method, anyone can learn a foreign language as long as he or she follows these explicit directions:

* Memorize the vocabulary on each page

* Follow that memorization by using a notecard to cover the words you have just memorized and test yourself.

* Then read the sentences following that are created from the vocabulary bank that you just mastered.

* Once fully memorized, give yourself the green light to proceed to the next page.

Again, if you proceed to the following page without mastering the previous, you are guaranteed to gain nothing from this book. If you follow the prescribed steps, you will realize just how effective and simplistic this method is.

THE PROGRAM

Let's Begin! "Vocabulary"
(memorize the vocabulary)

I | I am	Ana
With you	**(Masculine)** Ma'ak / **(Fem)** ma'keh
With him / with her	Ma'o / ma'a
With us	Ma'na
For you	**(Masculine)**La ilak/**(Feminine)**la ilik
Without him	Min duno
Without them	Min dunon
Always	Dayman
Was	Ken
This, This is, it is	Hayda
Today	Lyom
Sometimes	'Aw'aat
Maybe	Yimken
You/you are/are you	**(M)**Inta **(F)**inteh
Better	Ahsan / ahla
He/ he is	Huwweh
She/ she is	Heyyeh
From	Min

Sentences composed from the vocabulary (now you can speak the sentences and combine the words).

This is for you
Hayda ilak

I am from Lebanon
Ana min Libnen

Are you from Lebanon?
Inta min Libnen?

I am with you
Ana ma'ak

Sometimes you are with us at the mall
'Aw'aat enta ma'na bil mall

I am always with her
Ana dayman ma'a

Are you without them today?
Enta mish ma'on lyom?

Sometimes I am with him
'Aw'aat ana ma'o

*In Lebanese Arabic, there are gender rules. Saying "for you" to a male is *la ilak*, but if you are talking to a female, it's *la ilik*. *Kermalik* may be also used to signify "for you." "This is for you" means it belongs to you and, hence, in this case we use *ilak*. However, if the sentence was "I did it for you"(i.e., I did this only because you are a special friend to me or because you mean a lot to me), here in this context we use *kermehlik* for the girl and *kermehlak* for the boy.

17

I was	Ana kenet
To be	(M)Kun / (F)Kuni
The	El, le, l
Same	Nafs / Metel
Good	Mneeh
Here	Hon
Very	Kteer
And	Wa
Between	Bayn
Now	Halla'
Later / After / afterwards	Ba'den
If	Iza / La-w
Yes	Na'am / eh
To	A'l / la
Tomorrow	Bukra
Day	Yom
Also / too / as well	Kamen

If it's between now and later
Iza kenet bayn halla' wa ba'den
It's better tomorrow
Bukra ahsan
This is good as well
Hayda kamen mneh
To be the same person
Tay kuun nafs elshakhes
Yes, you are very good
Eh, inta kteer mneeh
I was here with them
Ana kenet hon ma'on
You and I
Inta w ana
The same day
Nafs el-yom

*In the Arabic language, adjectives usually proceed the noun. For example:
-"small house" / *beit zgheer*
-"tall person" / *shakhes taweel*
-"short person" / *shakhes 'a-seer*
There are exceptions, though. For example, when expressing admiration or something impressive, we can say, "How big is this house?" / *Shoo kbeer hal beit?*
*In Lebanese Arabic there are two forms to signify "if" / *iza* and *la-w.* "If it's raining tomorrow, I am not going," for instance, in this case, we use *"iza."* For "if I knew that this will happen, I wouldn't go to visit her," here the "if" is like "had I" and *la-w* will be used.

Me	Ana
Ok	Eh/ ok
Even if	Hatta la-w
No	La'a
Worse	Adrab
Where	Wein
Everything	Kilshi / Killon
Somewhere	B' Shimahal / Shimahal
What	Shu
Almost	Te'riban
There	Honeek
Is it? *(read footnote below)*	(M)Howa/(F)heya/(Ntr)hada

Afterwards is worse
Ba'dein adrab
Even if I go now
Hatta iza rehet halla'
Where is everything?
Wein kill-shi?
Maybe somewhere
Yimken b' shimahal / shimahal
What? I am almost there
Shu? Ana te'riban honeek
Where are you?
(M) Inta wein? / (F) Inteh wein?
Is it here?
Howa/heya/hada hon?

*In Arabic, the pronoun "me" has several definitions. In relation to verbs it's *neh* or *leh*. *Leh* refers to any verb that relates to the action of doing something to someone or for someone. For example, "tell me," "tell (to) me" / *Illeh*.
Ni just means "me": "love me" / *heb'neh* or "see me" / *shoof'neh*.
Other variations (*yeh, eh*):
-"on me" / *'aleyyeh*, "in me" / *fiyyeh*
-"to me" / *la 'eleh*, "with me" / *ma'eh*
-"in front of me" / *eddemeh*, "from me" / *minneh*
The same rule applies for "him" and "her"—both become suffixes: –*o* and –*a*.
Basically all verbs pertinent to males end with O, and all pertinent to female end with A.
-"love her" / *hebba*, "love him" / *hebbo*, "love them" / *hebbon*, "love us" / *hebbna*.
Any verb that relates to doing something to someone, or for someone put *l*:
-"tell her" / *illa*, "tell him" / *illo*, "tell them" / *il'lhun*, "tell us" /*il'linah*
Adding you as a suffix in Arabic is *ak* or *lak*, female *ik* or *lik*.
-"love you" / (M) *bhebbak* / (F)*bhebbik*, "tell you" / (M) *b'ellak* / (F) *b'ellik*
*In Arabic with the question "is it?", the "it" can pertain to either a masculine or feminine noun. However, whenever pertaining to a masculine or feminine noun, it will become *howa* or *heyaa*. For example, when referring to a feminine noun such as sayaara ("the car"), "is it (the car in question) here?" / *heya hon?* When referring to a masculine noun such as kaleb ("a dog"), "is it (the dog in question) on the table?" howa ala maida? For neuter, it's *hayda*. However, I yet again wish to stress that this n't a grammar book!

House	Beit
In / at	Be/ bill
Car	Seyyara
Already	Halla' / Saba' w
Good morning	Sabah el kheir
How are you?	(M) Kefak / (F) kefik
Where are you from?	Inta min wein?/(F)inteh min wein?
Impossible	Mustaheel
Hello	Marhaba
What is your name?	Shu ismak / shu ismik
How old are you?	(M)Addeh 'omrak/(F)Addeh 'omrik
Son	'Eben
Daughter	Benet
To have	(M) 'Endo / (F) 'Enda
Doesn't	Ma
Hard	So'eb *(difficult)* / Ehseh *(solid)*
Still	Ba'ed
Then *(or "so")*	Ye'neh

She doesn't have a car, so maybe she is still at the house?

Heyyeh ma 'enda seyyara, ye'neh yemkin heyyeh ba'da bill beit?

I am in the car already with your son and daughter

Ana bill seyyara hala ma'ah 'ebnak wa bentak

Good morning, how are you today?

Sabah el kheir, kefak lyom?

Hello, what is your name?

Marhaba, shu ismak?

How old are you?

Addeh 'omrak?

This is very hard, but it's not impossible

Haida kteer so'eb, bas mish mustaheel

Then where are you from?

Ye'neh min wein inta?

*In Arabic, possessive pronouns become suffixes to the noun. For example, in the translation for "your," *ak* is the masculine form, and *ik* is the feminine form.
-"your book" / *kteibak (m.), kteibik (f.)*
-"your house" / *beitak (m.), beitik (f.)*
*In the Arabic language, as well as in other Semitic languages, the article "a" doesn't exist. She doesn't have a car, *heya ma 'inda seyyara.*

Thank you	Shukran
For	La/ ala
Anything	Hayalla shi / 'Ay shi
That / That is	(M) Heyda / (F) Heydeh
Time	Wa'et
But	Bas / Leikin
No / Not	Ma, La' / mish, mish rah
I am not	Ana mish / ana manneh
Away	B'eed
Late	M'akhar
Similar	(M) Byishbaho / (F) Byishbaha
Another/ Other	Gheir/ teineh
Side	Janab/jehhut
Until	La-hadd / la
Yesterday	Mbeirih
Without us	Baleina / Be-dunna
Since	Min
Day	Yom
Before	'Abel

Thanks for everything
Shukran 'ala kill shi
It's almost time
Sar el wa'et te'reeban
I am not here, I am away
Ana mish hon, ana b'eed
That is a similar house
Hayda beit byishbaho
I am from the other side
Ana minel jehhut-teineh
But I was here until late yesterday
Bas ana kenet hon la mbeireh m'akhar
I am not at the other house
Ana manneh bil beit it-teineh

* In Lebanese Arabic, there are three definitions for time:
  -"time" / *wa't* refers to "era", "moment period," "duration of time."
  -"time(s)" / *marra(t)* refers to "occasion" or "frequency."
  -"time" / *sei'ah* references "hour," "what time is it?"
* In Lebanese Arabic, there are two separate cases used to signify "side": *janab* and *jehhut*. For "I am from the other side" *jehhut*, but for "I stand by your side" here "your side" is *janbak*.

21

I say / I am saying	Ana b'ool / ana 'am 'ool
What time is it?	Addeish-es le-sei'ah
I want	Ana baddeh
Without you	(M) Balak, Bidoonak /(F) balaki , bidoonik
Everywhere /wherever	Wein Makein
I go	Ana raayih, ana mehsheh/(F)raayha *(or)* mehshyeh
With	Ma'
My	Eleh
Cousin	(S)(M) Iben 'ammeh, (F) benet 'ammteh / (P)Wleid 'ammeh, baneit 'ammehteh
I need	Mehtej / ana bhajeh
Right now	Halla'
Night	Leil / 'ashiyyeh
To see	Shoof
Light	Noor / daw
Outside	Barra
Without	Bidoon / bala
Happy	Mabsoot
I see / I am seeing	Ana bshoof / ana shehyif

I am saying no / I say no
'Am ool la' / ana b'ool la'
I want to see this today
Ana baddeh shoof haydeh lyom
I am with you everywhere
Ana ma'ak wein makein
I am happy without my cousins here
Ana mabsoot bidoon wleid 'ammeh hon
I need to be there at night
Ana bhajeh koon honeek bill-leil
I see light outside
Ana sheyif daw barra
What time is it right now?
Addeish el-sei'ah halla'?

* "My" / eleh is also a possessive pronoun. Eleh means "my" but also becomes a suffix to a noun. Nouns ending in a vowel end with –teh. Nouns ending with a consonant end with –eh. For example:
-"cousin" / Iben el 'amm, "my cousin" / Iben 'ammeh
-"cup" / kibbeyeh, "my cup" / kibbeyteh
For second and third person masculine noun, *ibin* ("son"), male (s.) *ak*, (p.) *kom*, and female (s.) *ik*, (p.) *kum*. "His" – *Ilo* / "hers" – *ila*, noun endings will be o (for male) and a (for female). For example: "your son" / *ibn'ak* (m.), *ibnik* (f.), "your (plural) son" / *ibinkom* (m.), *bintkom* (f.), "his son" / *ibno*, "her son" / *ibna*, "our son" / *ibinn'a*, "their son" / *ibnon* (m.), *ibnon* (f.)
For second and third person feminine noun: "car" / *seyyara*. For example: "your car" / *seyyartak*, "your (plural) car" / *seyyaretkom*, "his car" / *seyyarto*, "her car" /*seyyareta*, "our car" / *seyyaretna*, "their car" / *seyyareton* (m.), *seyyareton* (f.)
* This *isn't* a phrase book! The purpose of this book is *solely* to provide you with the tool to create *your own* sentences!

Place	Makein / matrah
Easy	Hayyin /ba-seet /khafeef /sahill
To find	Tleh'ee
To look for/to search	Obrom / fattish
Near / Close	Areeb
To wait	Ntor
To sell	Baya'a
To use	Ista'amill
To know	A'ariff
To decide	Arrirr
Between	Bein
Both	Tneynehton
To	La / a'al
Next to	Hadde

This place it's easy to find
Haida matrah hayyin tleh'ee
I want to look for this next to the car
Ana baddeh obrom 'ala haydeh haddes - seyyara
I am saying to wait until tomorrow
Ana b'ool ntor la bukra
This table is easy to sell
Haydeh tawleh hayyin baya'a
I want to use this
Ana baddeh ista'amill haydeh
I need to know where is the house
Ana bhajeh a'ariff wein el-beit
I want to decide between both places
Ana baddeh arrirr bein matrahein

*Please pay close attention to the conjugation of verbs, whether they are in first person, second, or third. Unlike Anglo-Germanic languages, Latin languages, or even Classical Arabic, in which the first verb is conjugated and the following is always infinitive, in colloquial Arabic, it is quite different. The first verb is conjugated and the following one is conjugated as well. Keep in mind: The Lebanese dialect of the Arabic language is considered a colloquial, rather than an official language.

Because	La'enno / Kermeil
To buy	Ishtreh
They	Hinneh
Them, their	Elonn
Bottle	Anneeneh
Book	Kteib
Mine	La'ileh
To understand	Latifham
Problem / Problems	(S) Mashkal / (P) Mashehkill
I do / I am doing	Ba'amill
Of	Min
To look	Shehyif
Myself	Nefsi
Enough	Bikaffeh / sheb'oh
Food / water	Akill / ma-yy
Each/ every/ entire/ all	Kill / killon
Hotel	Otel

I like this hotel because I want to look at the beach
Ana bheb haydal otel la'anno baddeh shoof el-bahirr
I want to buy a bottle of water
Ana baddeh ishtreh anninett ma-yy
I do this every day
Ana ba'amill heik kill yom
Both of them have enough food
Tneynehton sheb'oh akill
That is the book, and that book is mine
Hayda huwweh l-kteib, w hayda l-kteib la'ileh
I need to understand the problem
Ana bhajeh ifham lMashkal
I see the view of the city from the hotel
Ana shehyif manzar l madineh min-el otel
I do my homework today
Ana'amm ba'amill fardeh lyom
My entire life (all my life)
Kill 'omreh / kill hayehteh

*"Both of them" / *tneynehton.*
*There are two ways of saying "life" in Arabic: *'omr* and *hayeht.*

I like	Ana bhebb
There is / There are	Fe
Family / Parents	'Ayleh / ahleh
Why	Lei / mishein
To say	Ool
Something	She
To go	Rooh
Ready	Jeh-his
Soon	Areeban
To work	Ishte-ghill
Who	Meen / yalleh
To know	A'aref
That (conjunction)	Inno

I like to be at my house with my parents
Ana bheb koon be beyteh ma' ahleh
I want to know why I need to say something important
Ana baddeh a'aref lei ana bhajeh ool she mhim
I am there with him
Ana honeek ma'o
I am busy, but I need to be ready soon
Ana mashghool, bass ana bhajeh koon jeh-his areeban
I like to go to work
Ana bhebb rooh ishte-ghill
'Who is there?
Meen honeek?
I want to know if they are here, because I want to go outside
Ana baddeh a'aref iza hinneh hon, la anno ana baddeh rooh la-barra
There are seven dolls
Fe saba' lei'aab
I need to know that it is a good idea
Ana bhajeh a'aref inno heydeh fekra mniha

*In the last sentence, we use "that" as a conjunction (*inno*)
and a demonstrative pronoun (M) *hayda* / (F) *heydeh*.
Ahla in colloquial Arabic slang is used to signify "great!"

How much /How many	Addeh
To bring	Jeeb
With me	Ma'eh
Instead	Badal
Only	Bas
When	Lamma
I can / Can I	Ana Fiyyeh *(or)* be'der
Or	Aw
Were	Kehno
Without me	Balehyeh / b-dooneh
Fast	Bser'aa
Slow	'A-mahill
Cold	Sa'aa
Inside	Joowweit
To eat	Ehcol
Hot	Sokhon/ hameh
To Drive	Soo'

How much money do I need to bring with me?
Addeh ana bhajeh jeeb ma'eh ma-sareh?
Instead of this cake, I want that cake
Badal hal gatto, baddeh hayda l-gatto
Only when you can
Bas lamma te'dirr
They were without me yesterday
Kehno Balehyeh mbehrih
Do I need to drive the car fast or slow?
Ana bhajeh soo' el seyyara bser'aa aw a-mahill?
It is cold inside the library
Fe sa'aa joowweit el-maktabeh
Yes, I like to eat this hot for my lunch
Eih, ana bhebb ehcol ghadeh'yeh sokhon
I can work today
Ana fiyyeh ishte-ghill lyom

*"Were" is *kehno,* "we were" is *kenna.*
*"I can" and "can I?" could either be *ana ader* or *ana fiyyeh.* "You can" or "can you?" is *te'dirr* or *feek?*

To answer	Jehwibb
To fly	Teer
Time / Times	Marra / Marrat
To travel	Sehfer
To learn	It'allam
How	Keef
To swim	Isbah
To practice	Timreen
To play	Il'aab
To leave	Khalleh
Many /much /a lot	Kteer (or) a'adad
I go to	Ana rooh 'ala
First	Awwal
Time / Times	Marra/Marrat

I want to answer many questions
Ana baddeh jehwibb 'aa-la as'ila kteereh
I must fly to Dubai today
Ana lehzim teer 'aa Dubai lyom
I need to learn how to swim at the pool
Ana bhajeh it'allam keef isbah bill berkeh
I want to learn to play better tennis
Ana baddeh it'allam il'aab tennis ahsan
I want to leave this here for you when I go to travel the world
Ana baddeh khalleh hayda hon la ilak lamma rooh sehfer el 'aalamm
Since the first time
Min awwal marra
The children are yours
Holeh wlehdak

*In Lebanese Arabic, "to leave (something)" is *khaleh.*
"To leave (a place)" is *tarak.*

*In Lebanese Arabic, there are three definitions for time:
- "time" / *wa't* refers to "era", "moment period," "duration of time."
- "time(s)" / *marra(t)* refers to "occasion" or "frequency."
- "time" / *seh'aa* references "hour," "what time is it?"

*With the knowledge you've gained so far, now try to create your own sentences!

Nobody / Anyone	Ma hada / hada
Against	Dodd
Us	Nehhna
To visit	Zoor
Mom / Mother	Mama, imm
To give	A'ateh
Which	Ayya
To meet	Tejtehme'
Someone	Hadah
Just	Bas
To walk	Timsheh
Around	Barmeh
Towards	Bittijehh
Than	Min
Nothing	Balashi / walashi

Something is better than nothing
Hal shi ahsan min balashi
I am against him
Ana dodo
Is there anyone here?
Fi hada hon?
We go to visit my family each week
Nehhna min rooh nzoor el ayleh kill jehm'aa
I need to give you something
Ana bhajeh a'teek shi
Do you want to go meet someone?
Baddak trooh tejtehme' ma' hadah?
I was here on Wednesdays as well
Ana kenet hon el orb'aa kamen
Do you do this everyday?
Enta bta'mel heik kill yom?
You need to walk around, but not towards the house
Enta bhajeh timsheh barmeh, bas mish bittijehh el-beit

*In Arabic, when using the pronoun "you" as a direct and indirect object pronoun (the person who is actually affected by the action that is being carried out) in relation to a verb, the pronoun "you" becomes a suffix to that verb. That suffix becomes *ak* (masc.) *ik* (fem.).
- "to give" / *ta'teh*: "to give you" / *a'teek*
- "to tell" / *ool*: "to tell you" / *Illak* (m.), *Illik* (f.)
- "see you" / *shoofak*: "to see you" (plural) / *shoofkon* (m.), *shoofkon* (f.)
For third person male, add *o* and *on* for plural, for female add *a* and *on* for plural.
- "tell him" / *Illo*
- "tell her" / *Illa*
- "see them" / *shoofon* (m.), *shoofon* (f.)
- "see us " / *shoofna*

I have	'Ehndeh
Don't	Ma
Friend	Saheb, sadee'
To borrow	Ist'eer
To look like / resemble	Ishbah
Grandfather	Jiddeh
To want	Baddeh
To stay	Ib'aa
To continue	Kammill
Way	Tari'
I don't	Manneh
To show	Tfarraj
To prepare	Hadderr
I am not going	Ana mishrah rooh
Like (preposition)	Metel

Do you want to look like Salim
Baddak tishbah Salim

I want to borrow this book for my grandfather
Ana baddeh Ist'eer hayda el ktehb la jiddeh

I want to drive and to continue on this way to my house
Ana baddeh soo' w kammill 'ala heydeh tari' la beiteh

I have a friend there, that's why I want to stay in Beirut
Ehndeh saheb honeek, mishein heik baddeh ib'a be beirut

I am not going to see anyone here
Ana mishrah rooh shoof hada hon

I need to show you how to prepare breakfast
Ana baddeh farjeek keef it'hadder terwee'a

Why don't you have the book?
Lei ma 'indak el-ktehb?

That is incorrect, I don't need the car today
Hayda mish mazboot, manneh bhajeh lal seyyara lyom

To remember	Titzakar
Your	Ilak
Number	Ra'em
Hour	Se'aa
Dark / darkness	'Atmeh
About / on the	'B-khsoos / ala
Grandmother	Sitteh
Five	Khams
Minute / Minutes	D'ee'ah / d'aye'
More	Aktar
To think	Fakker
To do	A'mel
To come	Ejeh
To hear	Esma'
Last	Ehkher

You need to remember my number
Enta bhajeh titzakar ra'emeh
This is the last hour of darkness
Haydeh ehkher Se'aa min el 'atmeh
I want to come and to hear my grandmother speak Arabic
Ana baddeh ejeh w esma' sitteh tehkeh 'arabeh
I need to think more about this, and what to do
Ana mehtej fakker b hayda aktar, w shoo a'mel
From here to there, it's only five minutes
Min hon la honeek, bas khams d'aye'
The school on the mountain
L maderseh ala l jabal

*In Lebanese Arabic b-khsoos is used to signify "about." For example, "let's talk about this topic" / ta nehkeh b-khsoos … "On the mountain" is a place, so in this case, we will use ala.

To leave	Yitrok
Again	Kamen /min jdeed
Syria	Suriyya
To take	Ehkhod
To try	Jarreb
To rent	Yista'jer
Without her	Bdoona
We are	Neh'na
To turn off	Taffeh
To ask	Tis'al
To stop	Nwa'iff
Permission	Ezin

He needs to leave and rent a house at the beach
Huwweh bhajeh yitrok w yista'jer beit a'la l baher
I want to take the test without her
Ana baddeh ehkhod l fahoss b-doona
We are here a long time
Nehna hon min zamen kteer
I need to turn off the lights early tonight
Ana bhajeh taffeh l odowyeh bakeer l leyleh
We want to stop here
Nehna badna nwa'iff hon
We are from Tripoli
Neh'na min Trabloss
The same building
Nafss el benehyeh
I want to ask permission to leave
Ana baddeh ekhod ezin la-itrok

*In Lebanese Arabic "to stop" is *twa'iff,* but to cease" is *khalas.*
For example, if someone is bothering you, you tell them STOP! / *Khalas.*

*In Lebanese dialect *kamen i*s frequently used to signify "again."
However, *min jdeed* and *marra tehneh* may be used as well.

To open	Iftah
A bit, a little, a little bit	Shwayyeh
To pay	Tidfa'
Once again	Tehneh marra
There isn't/ there aren't	Mafi
Sister	Okhteh
To hope	Bitmanna
To live	'Eesh
Nice to meet you	Tsharrafna bma'riftak
Name	Isem
Last name	Ism el 'ayleh
To return	Tirrja'
South	Jnub
Door	Beib

I need to open the door for my sister
Ana bhajeh iftah elbeib la okhteh
I need to buy something
Ana bhajeh ishtereh she
I want to meet your sisters
Ana baddeh 'abill okhtak
Nice to meet you, what is your name and your last name
Tsharrafna bma'riftak, shu ismak w isem 'ayltak?
To hope for a little better
Bitmanna shi shwey ahsan
I want to return from the United States and to live in Qatar without problems
Ana baddeh irja' min Amrika w 'eesh b Qatar bala mashehkill
Why are you sad right now?
(M)Lei inta hazeen halla'? (F) Lei inteh hazeeneh halla'?
There aren't any people here
Ma-fe nehss hon
There isn't enough time to go to South Lebanon today
Ma-fe kfeyeh wa'et lal rawha 'a jnub lebnein lyom

*In Lebanese Arabic "nice to meet you" for masculine case is
tsharrafna bma'riftak, and for feminine case is *tsharrafna bma'riftik.*
*This *isn't* a phrase book! The purpose of this book is *solely* to provide
you with the tools to create *your own* sentences!

To happen	Yehsal
To order	Otlob
To drink	Ishrab
Excuse me	Bill ezin
Child	(M) Ebneh, (F) Binteh
Woman	Mara
To begin / To start	Ballish
To finish	Khalliss
To help	Seh'ed
To smoke	Dakhin
To love	Hebb
To talk / To Speak	Eh'keh

This must happen today
Hayda lehzim yehsal lyom
Excuse me, my child is here as well
Bill ezin, ibneh honeh kamen
I love you
Ana bhebbak
I see you
Ana sheyfak
I need you at my side
Ana bhajeh ilak haddeh
I need to begin soon to be able to finish at 3 o'clock in the afternoon
Ana bhajeh ballish areeban hatta khalliss 'a seh'a tlehteh ba'd el dohor
I need help
Ana bhajeh la museh'adeh
I don't want to smoke once again
Ana ma baddeh dakhin tehneh marra
I want to learn how to speak Arabic
Ana baddeh it'allam keef eh'keh 'arabeh

*"To help" is sa'ed. However, "help!" is *museh'adeh*.
"I need help" or "I need rescue" / *ana mahtej le museh'adeh*.
*"To be able to" is *hatta*.

To read	Ii'ra
To write	Iktob
To teach	'Allem
To close	Sakkir
To choose	Ikhtar
To prefer	Bfaddill
To put	Hott
Less	A'el
Sun	Shamess
Month	Shaher
I Talk	Behkeh
Exact	Mazbut

I need this book to learn how to read and write in Arabic because I want to teach in Egypt
Ana bhajeh la hayda likteib ta it'allam kif ii'ra w iktub bill-'arabeh la 'inno baddeh 'allem bi ma-ser
I want to close the door of the house
Ana baddeh sakkir beib el-beit
I prefer to put the gift here
Ana bfaddill hott el hdiyeh hon
I want to pay less than you for the dinner
Ana baddeh idfa' a'el minnak bill 'asha
I speak with the boy and the girl in French
Ana behkeh ma' el' sabeh will benett bill frinsehweh
There is sun outside today
Fi shamess barra lyom
Is it possible to know the exact date?
Mumkin ma'rfitt tehrikh el mazbut?

*"In" is *bill*.

*"For the" is *li*

*With the knowledge you've gained so far, now try to create your own sentences!

34

To exchange (*money*)	Osrof
To call	Otto-sill
Brother	Khayyeh
Dad	Bayyeh
To sit	E'e'od
Together	Sawa
To change	T'ghayyer
Of course	Akeed
Welcome	Ahlein
During	Wa'et
Years	(S)Seneh / (P)Sneen
Sky	Sama
Up	Fo'
Down	Tahet
Sorry	Be'tezirr
To follow	Ilha'
To the	Ila
Big	Kbeer
New	Jedid
Never / ever	Abadan

I don't want to exchange this money at the bank
Ana ma baddeh osrof hal mahsareh bill-bank
I want to call my brother and my dad today
Ana baddeh otto-sill b-khayyeh wbayyeh lyom
Of course I can come to the theater, and I want to sit together with you and with your sister
Akeed ana be'dir ejeh a'l massrah, w ana baddeh e'e'od sawa ma'ak w ma' okhtak
I need to go down to see your new house
Ana bhajeh inzal la tahet ta shoof beytik el jdeed
I can see the sky from the window
Ana adirr shoof e'sama min el shibbeik
I am sorry, but he wants to follow her to the store
Ana be'tezirr, bass baddeh ilha'a 'al mahal
I don't ever want to see you again
Abadan ma baddeh shoofik marra tehneh

*In Lebanese dialect, brother is *khay,* and dad is *bay.* However, "my dad" is *bayyeh,* and "my brother" is *khayyeh.* "My sister" is *okhteh,* and "my mother" is *immeh .*
*For the possessive pronouns, her (*ha*) and him (*hu*), both become suffixes to the verb or noun. Concerning nouns: her house / *beita*, his house / *beito*, concerning cases regarding verbs, please see footnotes on page #19.

To allow	Khallee
To believe	Bsadde'
Morning	'Abookra
Except	Min-'ada
To promise	Boo'dak
Good night	Tisbah 'a kheir
Street	Shehri
People	Neis
To move	In'ol
Far	B'eed
Different	Gheir
Man	Rijjel
To enter	Foot
To receive	Istelim
Throughout	Khileil
Good afternoon	Ma-sa el kheir
Left / right	Shmel / yameen
Him / Her	Huwweh / heyyeh

I need to allow him to go with us, he is a different man now
Ana bhajeh khallee yrooh ma'na, la'enno huwweh gheirrijjel halla'
I believe everything except this
Ana bsadde' kill-shi min'ada haydeh
I promise to say good night to my parents each night
Ana boo'dak inno 'ool tisbah 'a kheir la ahleh kill leyleh
The people from Jordan are very pleasant
El neiss bill ordon kteer lutafa
I need to find another hotel very quickly
Ana bhajeh leh'eh otel tehneh be'ser'a
They need to receive a book for work
Hinneh bhajeh yistelmo kteib lal sheghill
I see the sun in the morning
Ana bshoof sh shamess 'abookra
The house is on the right side of the street
El beit huwweh 'a yehmeen el shehri'

To wish	Itmanna
Bad	Aa'tel/ ma mneeh
To Get	Yekhod
To forget	Insa
Everybody / Everyone	Kill shakhess/ killon
Although	Ma' inno
To feel	Hiss
Great	Mhim
Next(as in close, near)	Hadd
To like	Bhibb
In front	Iddeim
Person	Shakhes
Behind	Wara
Well	Ahsan
Goodbye	Bye
Restaurant	Mat'aam
Bathroom	Hemmeim
Next (as in next year)	Jei

I don't want to wish you anything bad
Ana ma baddeh itmanneilak ayya shi aa'tel

I must forget everybody from my past to feel well
Ana leizim insa kill shakess min el madeh hatta
hiss ahsan

I am next to the person behind you
Ana hadd el shakhes yalleh warak

There is a great person in front of me
Fi shakhes mhim iddeimeh

I say goodbye to my friends
Ana b'oul bye la rif'ateh

Where is the bathroom in the restaurant?
Wein el hemmeim bill mat'aam?

She has to get a car before the next year
Heya lehzim tjeeb seyyara abel sint el jei

I like the house, but it is very small
Ana bheb el beit, bass huwweh kteer zgheer

Hadd literally means "side." In Lebanese Arabic, it's also used to signify "next." *Haddeh* is "besides me" and *haddak* is "besides you".

To remove / to take out	Tsheel
Please	'Mol ma'roof
Beautiful	(M)Helo/(F)helweh
To lift	Ish'ol
Include / Including	Ma'
Belong	Byedkhol
To hold	Timsok
To check	It'akkad
Small	Zgheer
Real	Ha'ee'eh
Week	Jem'aa
Size	Kebirr
Even though	Hatta la-w
Doesn't	Mish
So (as in "then")	Ye'neh
So (as in "so big")	Kteer
Price	Se'haer

She wants to remove this door please
Hiyyeh badda tsheel hal beib 'mol ma'roof
This doesn't belong here, I need to check again
Hayda ma byedkhol hon, ana bhajeh it'akkad kamein
This week the weather was very beautiful
Hal Jem'aa el ta'ess kein kteer helo
I need to know which is the real diamond
Ana bhajeh a'ref ayya elmazhuwweh ha'ee'eh
We need to check the size of the house
Nehna bhajeh nit'akkad min kibr el beit
I want to lift this, so you need to hold it high
Ana baddeh ish'ol hayda, ye'neh leizim timseko bill 'aleh
I can pay this even though that the price is expensive
Ana eider idfa' hayda hatta la w inno el se'er ghaleh
Including everything is this price correct?
Ma' kill shi hass se'er mazboot?

Countries of the Middle East
Bildein el-shar' el- awsatt

Lebanon	Lebnein
Syria	Suriyya
Jordan	L-ordon
Israel/Palestine/West Bank	Isra'eel/folosteen/deffeh el-gharbeyyeh
Iraq	L-'Ira'
Saudi Arabia	So'odiyyeh
Kuwait	L-Kweit
Qatar	Qatar
Bahrain	L-Bahrein
United Arab Emirates	L-Emarat
Oman	'Oman
Yemen	L-Yaman
Egypt	Mossor
Libya	Leebya
Tunisia	Tunis
Algeria	L-Jazeh'ir
Morocco	Maghreb

Months

January	Kenoon el tehneh
February	Shbatt
March	Adar
April	Nissein
May	Ayyar
June	Hzeyran
July	Tammooz
August	Ab
September	Aylool
October	Teshreen el awwal
November	Teshreen el tehneh
December	Kenoon el awwal

Days of the Week

Sunday	Ahad
Monday	Tanein
Tuesday	Taleita
Wednesday	Orb'aa
Thursday	Khamees
Friday	Jem'aa
Saturday	Sabet

Seasons

Spring	Rabee'
Summer	Seif
Autumn	Khareef
Winter	Shehteh

Cardinal Directions

North	Shmeil
South	Jnoob
East	Share'
West	Ghareb

Colors

Black	(M)Aswad (F)Sawda
White	(M)Abyadd (F)Bayda
Gray	(M)Rmehdeh (F)Rmehdiyyeh
Red	(M)Ahmar (F)Hamra
Blue	(M)Azra (F)Zar'a
Yellow	(M)Asfar (F)Safra
Green	(M)Akhdar (F)Khadra
Orange	Berd'aneh
Purple	Leylakeh
Brown	(M)Benne (F)Benniyye

Numbers

One	Wahad
Two	Tnein
Three	Tleteh
Four	Arb'aa
Five	Khamseh
Six	Sitteh
Seven	Sab'aa
Eight	Tmehneh
Nine	Tis'aa
Ten	'Ashra

Twenty	'Eshreen
Thirty	Tlehteen
Forty	Arb'aaeen
Fifty	Khamseen
Sixty	Sitteen
Seventy	Saba'aeen
Eighty	Tmaneen
Ninety	Tisi'in
Hundred	Miyyeh
Thousand	Alef
Million	Malyoon

Conversational
Arabic
Quick and Easy

PALESTINIAN DIALECT

YATIR NITZANY

THE PALESTINIAN ARABIC DIALECT

Palestinian Arabic, like many other Middle Eastern languages, is a dialect of the more official Modern Standard Arabic language. However, though various countries have their own dialects, Palestinian Arabic is most similar to Syrian and Lebanese Arabic and is considered a Levantine dialect, named after the Levant region that encompasses Jordan, Syria, Israel, Palestine, Lebanon, Cyprus, and Turkey's Hatay province. This dialect is spoken throughout the Palestinian territories (West Bank and Gaza) as well as among the Arab citizens of Israel. The Palestinian dialect varies slightly throughout each area and city of Palestine and Israel. With this language, the urban versions are surprisingly not as popular as its rural versions, though urban versions are slowly growing.

Spoken in: Palestine and Israel

ARABIC PRONUNCIATIONS

PLEASE MASTER THE FOLLOWING PAGE IN ARABIC PRONUNCIATIONS PRIOR TO STARTING THE PROGRAM

Kha. For Middle Eastern languages including Arabic, Hebrew, Farsi, Pashto, Urdu, Hindi, etc., and also German, to properly pronounce the kh or ch is essential, for example, *Khaled* (a Muslim name) or *Chanukah* (a Jewish holiday) or *Nacht* ("night" in German). The best way to describe kh or ch is to say "ka" or "ha" while at the same time putting your tongue at the back of your throat and blowing air. It's pronounced similarly to the sound that you make when clearing your throat. Please remember this whenever you come across any word containing a *kh* in this program.

Ghayin. The Arabic *gh* is equivalent to the "g" in English, but its pronunciation more closely resembles the French "r," rather than "g." Pronounce it at the back of your throat. The sound is equivalent to what you would make when gargling water. Gha is pronounced more as "rha," rather than as "ga." *Ghada* is pronounced as "rhada." In this program, the symbol for *ghayin* is *gh*, so keep your eyes peeled.

Aayin is pronounced as a'a, pronounced deep at the back of your throat. Rather similar to the sound one would make when gagging. In the program, the symbol for *aayin* is a'a, u'u, o'o, or i'i.

Ha is pronounced as "*ha.*" Pronunciation takes place deep at the back of your throat, and for correct pronunciation, one must constrict the back of the throat and exhale air while simultaneously saying "ha." In the program, this strong h ("*ha*") is emphasized whenever *ha, ah, hi, he,* or *hu* is encountered.

NOTE TO THE READER

The purpose of this book is merely to enable you to communicate in Palestinian Arabic. In the program itself (pages 17-39) you may notice that the composition of some of those sentences might sound rather clumsy. This is intentional. These sentences were formulated in a specific way to serve two purposes: to facilitate the easy memorization of the vocabulary and to teach you how to combine the words in order to form your own sentences for quick and easy communication, rather than making complete literal sense in the English language. So keep in mind that this is not a phrase book!

As the title suggests, the sole purpose of this program is for conversational use only. It is based on the mirror translation technique. These sentences, as well as the translations are not incorrect, just a little clumsy. Latin languages, Semitic languages, and Anglo-Germanic languages, as well as a few others, are compatible with the mirror translation technique.

Many users say that this method surpasses any other known language learning technique that is currently out there on the market. Just stick with the program and you will achieve wonders!

Again, I wish to stress this program is by no means, shape, or form a phrase book! The sole purpose of this book is to give you a fundamental platform to enable you to connect certain words to become conversational. Please also read the "Introduction" and the "About Me" section prior to commencing the program.

In order to succeed with my method, please start on the very first page of the program and fully master one page at a time prior to proceeding to the next. Otherwise, you will overwhelm yourself and fail. Please do not skip pages, nor start from the middle of the book.

It is a myth that certain people are born with the talent to learn a language, and this book disproves that myth. With this method, anyone can learn a foreign language as long as he or she follows these explicit directions:

* Memorize the vocabulary on each page

* Follow that memorization by using a notecard to cover the words you have just memorized and test yourself.

* Then read the sentences following that are created from the vocabulary bank that you just mastered.

* Once fully memorized, give yourself the green light to proceed to the next page.

Again, if you proceed to the following page without mastering the previous, you are guaranteed to gain nothing from this book. If you follow the prescribed steps, you will realize just how effective and simplistic this method is.

THE PROGRAM

Let's Begin! "Vocabulary"
(memorize the vocabulary)

I, I am	Ana
With you	Ma'ak / ma'aki
With him / with her	Ma'au / Ma'aha
With us	Ma'ana
For you	(**Masc**) Ilak / (**Fem**) Ilha
Without him	Bidunu
Without them	Bidunhum / mish ma'ahum
Always	Da'iman / Ala tul
Was	Kan
This, This is	Hada
It, It's	Hada
Sometimes	Ahyanan
Maybe	Yimkin
Are you	(**M**)Hal inta,(**F**)hal inti
Better	Ahsan
You, you are	(**M**)Inta/ (**F**)inti
He, he is /She, she is	Hou/Hiyya
From	Min
Today	Ilyum

Sentences from the vocabulary (now you can speak the sentences and connect the words)

I am with you
Ana ma'ak

This is for you
Hada ilak

I am from Palestine
Ana min Falastin

Are you from Ramallah?
Inta min Ram-allah?

Sometimes you are with us at the mall
Ahyanan inta bitkun ma'na fi al mall

I am always with her
Ana da'iman ma'ha

Are you without them today?
Inta bidunhum ilyum?

Sometimes I am with him
Ahyanan bakun ma'u

*In Palestinian Arabic, there are gender rules. Saying "for you" to a male is *ilak*, but if you are talking to a female, then it's *ilik*.

*In spoken Arabic, words like *hal* / "are" are usually dropped, and we only say, *Hiyya aklat? Huwwa Nayim?*, etc., which, if written in Classical Arabic, would have been, *Hal akalat hiya?* or *Hal huwa Na'im?*

I was	Ana kunt
To be	(M)Ykun / (F) Itkun
The	Al/ il/ l'
Same / like (as in similar)	Nafs, nafs ilshi / mithl
Good	Mnih
Here	Hawn
Very	Ktir
And	Wa
Between	Bain
Now	Halqait/ Hala
Later / After / afterwards	Ba'dain
If	Iza/In
Yes	Ah / Aywah
To	La
Tomorrow	Bukra
Person	Shakhs / wahad
Also / too / as well	Kaman

If it was between now and later
Iza kan hada bain halla' wu ba'dain
It's better tomorrow
Ahsan *or* Afdal bukra
This is good as well
Hada kaman mnih
To be the same person
Ykun nafs ishakhs
Yes, you are very good
Ah, inta mnih ktir
I was here with them
Ana kunt hawn ma'ahum
You and I
Inta wa ana
The same day
Nafs ilyum

*In the Arabic language, adjectives follow the noun. For example, "the same day" is *nafs ilyum*, "small house" is *beit zrir,* "tall person" is *asha'khis tawil,* and "short person" is *asha'khis aseer.*

*In this program the article "the/*al, il, l'* will sometimes become a suffix at the beginning of the noun. For nouns beginning with *d, n, r, s, sh, t, th,* and *z,* the *l* is omitted and replaced with the initial consonant of the following noun. "The people" / *al-shakhs* is *ashakhs.* "The Nile" / *al-nil* is *an-nil.* It is dropped when spoken; however, when written, it's usually *al-shaks or al-nil.*

Me	Ana
Ok	Tayyib
Even if	Hatta lau
No	Ma / la
Worse	Al'an / aswa'a
Where	Wain
Everything	Kulshi / Kulluh
Somewhere	Fi mahal / Fi makan
What	Ish, shu
Almost	Taqriban / ta'riban
There	Hinak
I go	Ana baruh/Ana bamshi

Afterwards is worse
Ba'dain biykun aswa'a [or] al'an
Even if I go now
Hatta lau ana ruht halqait
Where is everything?
Wain kul ilashya'a
Maybe somewhere
Yimkin bimahal
What? I am almost at home
Ish? Ana ta'riban fi bayt
Where are you?
Wainak? / inta wain?

*Fi makan literally means "in a place."
*Since Palestinian Arabic isn't an official language but rather a colloquial dialect, we are using grammar rules from Classical Arabic. In the Arabic language, the pronoun "me" has several forms. When it is attached to verbs, it is pronounced "nee."
For example, "help me" is saaednee. Lee is the preposition (to + the pronoun "me"), and it refers to any verb that is about an action of doing/giving something to someone. For example, "tell me" is qul lee. "Tell him" is qul laho. "Tell her" is qul laha. "Tell them" is qul lahom if masculine plural and qul lahonna if feminine plural. "Tell us" is qul lana.
The same rule applies for other pronouns that become suffixes. "Bring her" is ahderha. "Bring him" is ahderho. "Bring them" is ahderhom. "Bring us" is ahderna.
*Ana baruh / Ana bamshi can be used to signify both male and female cases, as well as future and present tenses.

House	Bait
In, at, at the	Bil/ fi/fil
Car	Sayarrah
Already	Khalas
Good morning	Sabah al khir
How are you?	Kifak / kif ilhal/kifik [for female]
Where are you from?	Inta min wain? / Inti min wain?
Today	Ilyum
Hello	Marhaba
What is your name?	Shu ismak / Ish ismik [for Female]?
How old are you?	Kaddaish umrak? / kaddaish umrik?
Son	Ibin
Daughter	Bint
To have	Yikun induh/indha[female]
Doesn't	Ma
Hard	Si'ib
Still	Lissah
Impossible	Mustahil

She doesn't have a car, so maybe she is still at the house?
Hiyya ma indha sayarah, ya'ni yimkin lissat-ha fil bait
I am in the car now with your son and daughter
Ana halqait fil sayarah ma' ibnak wi bintak
Good morning, how are you today?
Sabah al-khir, kifak ilyum? [or] Kif halak ilyum?
Hello, what is your name?
Marhaba, ish ismik/shu ismak?
How old are you?
Kaddaish Umrak?
This is very hard, but it's not impossible
Hada ktir si'ib bas mish mustahil
Where are you from?
Min wain inta?

*In Arabic, possessive pronouns become suffixes to the noun. For example, for the English word "your," ak is the masculine form, and ik is the feminine form.
* "your book" / ktabak (m.), ktabik (f.)
* "your house" / baitak (m.), baitik (f.)
*In the Arabic language, as well as in other Semitic languages the article "a" doesn't exist. "She doesn't have a car" / hiyya ma indha sayarah.
*The definition of khalas can also mean "done" or "finished."

Thank you	Shukran
For	Ala
Anything	Ay-shi
That, That is	Hada
Time	Waqit
But	Bas / lakin
Not	Ma, La / mish
I am not	Ana mish
Away	Bi'id
Late	Mit'akhir
Similar	Biyishbahu, zay ba'ad
Another/other	Wahad Tani/ghair
Side	Janb / taraf
Until	Lahad
Yesterday	Imbarih
Without us	Bidunna
Since	Min
Day	Yum
Before	Abil/qabil

Thanks for anything
Shukran ala ay shi
I am not here
Ana mish hun
That is a similar house
Hadak ilbait biyishbahu
I am from the other side
Ana min iltaraf iltani
But I was here until late yesterday
Bas ana kunt hun lahad waqit mit'akhir imbarih
I am not at the other house
Ana mish fil bait eltani

In Arabic there are 3 definitions for time:
Time, *waqt* refers to; era, moment period, duration of time.
Time(s), *marra(t)* refers to; occasion or frequency.
Time, *sa'a* in reference to; hour, what time is it.

I say / I am saying	Ana baqul/ ana ba'ul / ul
What time is it?	Qaddish ilsi'ah?
I want	Ana biddi
Without you	Bidunak / balak
Everywhere /wherever	Fi kul makan/ Fi ay makan
I am going	(M)Ana rayih,ana mashi/(F)ana rayha,ana mashia
With	Ma'a
My	Ili
Cousin	(M)Ibn il'am (or) Ibn ilkhal [uncle from mother's side), (P)Wlad il'am /wlad ilkhal (F)bint il'am/ bint ilkhal, (P)banat il'am, banat ilkhal
I need	Mihtaj, lazim
Right now	Halqait
Night	Lail
To see	Ashuf
Light	Daw
Outside	Barra
Without	Bidun / Bala
Happy	Mabsut
I see / I am seeing	Ana shayif

I am saying no / I say no
Ana baqul la' / ana ba'ul la'
I want to see this today
Ana biddi ashuf hada ilyum
I am with you everywhere
Ana ma'ak fi kul makan
I am happy without my cousins here
Ana mabsut bidun wlad ammi hawn
I need to be there at night
Ana lazim akun hinak bil lail
I see light outside
Ana shayif daw barrah
What time is it right now?
Qaddaish ilsaa halqait/halla?

*Since Palestinian Arabic isn't an official language, but rather a colloquial dialect, we are using grammar rules from Classical Arabic. "My" is a possessive pronoun that comes as a suffix to a noun (ee) in Arabic. For example, "father" is ab while "my father" is abee. "Cup" is koob while "my cup" is koobee.

For second and third person, "your father" is abooka if masculine, and abookee if feminine. "Your father" (plural) is abookom if masculine plural, and abookonna if feminine plural. "His father" is aboho. "Her father" is aboha. "Their father" is abohom if masculine and aboohonna if feminine. "Our father" is abona.

* "your car" / sayart'ak, "your (plural) car" / sayart'akum, sayart'akun
* "his car" / sayart'hu, "her car" / sayart'ha
* "our car" / sayart'naa, "their car" / sayart'hum (m.), sayart'hun (f.)

*This isn't a phrase book! The purpose of this book is solely to provide you with the tools to create your own sentences!

Place	Makan, mahl
Easy	Hayyin, basit, khafif, sahil
To find	Itlaqi
To look for/to search	Addawir
Near / Close	Qarib/Arib/janb
To wait	Yistanna
To sell	Yabi'i/itbi'I [F]
To use	Asta'mail
To know	A'rif
To decide	Aqarrir
Between	Bain
Both	Litnain
To	Ila / Ala

This place is easy to find
Sahil itlaqi hada ilmakan
I want to look for this near the car
Ana biddi addawir ala hada janb ilsayarra
I am saying to wait until tomorrow
Ana ba'ul/baqul nistana lahad bukra
This table is easy to sell
Hadi iltawlah sahil bayha
I want to use this
Biddi asta'mil hada
I need to know where is the house
Mihtaj a'rif wain ilbait
I want to decide between both places
Ana biddi aqarrir bain ilmahallain

*Please pay close attention to the conjugation of verbs, whether they are in first person, second, or third. Unlike Anglo-Germanic languages, Latin languages, or even Classical Arabic, in which the first verb is conjugated and the following is always infinitive, in colloquial Arabic, it is quite different. The first verb is conjugated and the following verb is conjugated as well. Keep in mind the Palestinian dialect of the Arabic language is considered a colloquial, rather than an official language.

*Janb literally means "side."

Because	Ashan/li'annuh
To buy	Ashtri
Life	Hayat, Umr
Them, They	Humma
Bottle	Qanninah/Anninah
Book	Ktab
Mine	Taba'i/ li
To understand	Afham
Problem / Problems	Mushkilah/mashakil
I do / I am doing	Ana ba'mil / Ana bassawi
Of	Min
To look	Ashuf / Yttalla'a
Myself	Bnafsi
Enough	Bikfi/khalas
Food / water	Akil / mai
Each/ every/ entire/ all	Kul wahad/ilkul/kulhum/kul
Hotel	Autail

I like this hotel because I want to look at the beach
Ana bahib hada ilautail li'annu biddi ashuf elshat

I want to buy a bottle of water
Ana biddi ashtri anninat [or qanninat] mai

I do this every day
Ana ba'mil haik kul yum

Both of them have enough food
Ilitnain indhum akil kafi

That is the book, and that book is mine
Hada hu liktab, wihada liktab taba'i

I need to understand the problem
Ana mihtaj afham ilmushkilah

I see the view of the city from the hotel
Ana bashuf manzar ilmadinah min il autail

I am going to do my homework today
Ana rah a'mil wajbi ilmanzili ilyum

My entire life (all my life)
Kul umri/kul hayati

*"At the" is *le*
*"Both of them" is *Tneinetoun*
*There are two ways of saying "life" in Arabic: *o'omr* and *hayat*.
Haik means "this way," "in this manner," or "like this."

54

I like	Bahib / ajib
There is / There are	Fi
Family / Parents	Ahil/elwaldain
Why	Laish
To say	Aqul/A'ul
Something	Ishi
To go	Aruh
Ready	Jahiz
Soon	Qarib
To work	Ashtighil
Who	Min
To know	Yi'rif
That (conjunction)	Innu
Idea	Fikra

I like to be at my house with my parents
Bahib akun fi baiti ma'a ahli [Ummi wa abuy]
I want to know why I need to say something important
Ana badi a'rif laish lazim aqul/a'ul ishi muhim
I am there with him
Ana hinak ma'uh
I am busy, but I need to be ready soon
Ana mashgul, bas lazim ajhaz bisur'a
I like to go to work
Bahib aruh ala ilshughul
Who is there?
Min hinak?
I want to know if they are here, because I want to go outside
Biddi a'rif iza kanu mawjudin hawn, li'an biddi atla'a barra
There are seven dolls
Fi Sabi' Lu'ab
I need to know that that is a good idea
Biddi a'rif innu hadi fikrah mniha

*In the last sentence, we use "that" as a conjunction *(inou)*
and as a demonstrative pronoun *(haida).*
*The definition of *ummi wa abuy* is "my mom and my dad."
Kanu mawjudin means "present."
Atla'a means "go out" or "leave" or "go up."

How much /How many	Qaddish? Addish?
To bring	Ajib
With me	Ma'ai
Instead	Badal
Only	Bas
When	Lamma
I can / Can I?	Ana Baqdar, ba'dar/ Baqdar?
Or	Aw / willa
Were	Kan
Without me	Biduni/min ghairi
Fast	Sari'i
Slow	Bati'i
Cold	Barid
Inside	Juwwa
To eat	Akul
Hot	Sukhun
To Drive	Asuq/asu'

How much money do I need to bring with me?
Qaddish [Addish] masari lazim ajib ma'i?
Instead of this cake, I want that cake
Badal hadi ilka'ka biddi hadik ilka'ka
Only when you can
Bas lamma tiqdar [ti'dar]
They were without me yesterday
Kanu min ghairi imbarih
Do I need to drive the car fast or slow?
Lazim asuq ilsayara bisur'ah willa bati'i?
It is cold inside the library
Iljaw barid juwwa ilmaktaba
Yes, I like to eat this hot for my lunch
Ah, ana bahib akul shi sukhun haik ala ilghada
I can work today
Ana baqdar [ba'dar] ashtighil ilyum

*I can and can I, could either be *ana qader* or *ana baqdar*. You can or can you? is *tiqdar [ti'dar]*.

*Were, kan but *they were,* add the suffix to the pronoun *Kanu*. We were is *Kunna*.

56

To answer	Ajawib
To fly	Atir
Time / Times	Marra / Marrat
To travel	Asafir
To learn	Ata'alam
How	Kif
To swim	Asbah
To practice	Itmarran
To play	Al'ab
To leave (something)	Akhalli
Many /much /a lot	Adad kbir/ktir/Kammiyah kbirah
I go to	Ana baruh ala
First	Awwal
Time / Times	Waqt/Wa't, Awqat/Aw'at *or* zaman
Around	Hawl

I want to answer many questions
Ana biddi ajawib ala as'ila ktira
I must fly to Dubai today
Ana lazim atir ala Dubai ilyum
I need to learn how to swim at the pool
Ana lazim at'alam kif asbah fil birkah
I want to learn to play better tennis
Ana badi ata'alam al'ab tennis mnih
I want to leave this here for you when I travel around the world
Biddi akhalli hada hun ilak lamma asafir hawl elalam
Since the first time
Min awwal marra
The children are yours
Ilawlad ilak

*In Arabic there are 3 definitions for time:
Time, *waqt* refers to; era, moment period, duration of time.
Time(s), *marra(t)* refers to; occasion or frequency.
Time, *sa'a* in reference to; hour, what time is it.

*In Palestinian Arabic; *to leave* (something) is *yikhalli*.
  To leave (a place) is *Yitrik*.

Nobody / Anyone	Walahada/ayhada
Against	Dud
Us	Nihna
To visit	Azur
Mom / Mother	Mama, im
To give	A'ti
Which	Ayy
To meet	Itqabil/itabil
Someone	Wahad
Just	Bas
To walk	Amshi
Week	Usbu'u or jum'a
Towards	Jihhit
Than	Min
Nothing	Balash/ wala shi

Something is better than nothing
Ayshi ahsan min balash
I am against her
Ana dud-ha
We go to visit my family each week
Nihna min ruh inzur ahli kul jum'a (also kul usbu'u)
I need to give you something
Ana mihtaj a'tik shi
Do you want to go meet someone?
Biddak truh itqabil/itabil ahad?
I was here on Wednesdays as well
Ana kunt hun Kaman yum ilarba'a
Do you do this everyday?
Inta bitsawi haik kul yum?
You need to walk, but not towards the house
Inta mihtaj titmasha, bas mish bittijah ilbait

*Since Palestinian Arabic isn't an official language, but rather a colloquial dialect, we are using grammar rules from Classical Arabic. In Arabic, when using the pronoun "you" as a suffix—*ka* or *laka* if masculine, *kee* or *lakee* if feminine—the pronoun is actually used as a direct and indirect object pronoun (the person who is actually affected by the action that is being carried out). In relation to a verb, the pronoun "you" becomes a suffix to that verb. "I love you" is *aohebboka* if masculine and *aohebbokee* if feminine. "I tell you" is *aqulo laka* if masculine and *aqulo lakee* if feminine. For a third person, "I tell you" is *aqulo lakom* if masculine plural and *aqulo lakonna* if feminine plural.
*The definition of *bitsawi haik* is "do this."

I have	Indi
Don't	Ma
Friend	Sahib, Sadi'/Sadiq
To borrow	Asta'ir / Yitddayan
To look like / resemble	Byishbah
Grandfather	Jid/sid
To want	Biddu/biddi/bidha
To stay	Abqa
To continue	Akkamil
Way (road, path)	Tariq/tari', mamar
Way (method)	Tariqa/tari'a
I dont	Ana ma
To show	Yifarji, yiwaddih
To prepare	Itjahiz/Ahaddir
I am not going	Ana mish (M)rayih/(F)rayha
To do	A'amil

Do you want to look like Salim
Biddak tishbah Salim?

I want to borrow this book for my grandfather
Ana biddi asta'ir hada liktab la jiddi/la sidi

I want to drive and to continue on this way to my house
Ana biddi asouq wa akkamil ala hada iltariq labaiti

This isn't the way to do this
Hadi mish tariqit [tari'it] amalha

I have a friend there, that's why I want to stay in Jerusalem
Anda indi sahib hinak, ashan haik biddi abqa fi Alquds

I am not going to see anyone here
Ana mish rah ashuf hadan hun

I need to show you how to prepare breakfast
Biddi awarrik kif itjahiz liftur

Why don't you have that book?
Laish ma indak hada liktab?

That is incorrect, I don't need the car today
Hada Mish mazbut. Ana mish mihtaj ilsayarah ilyum

*Mazbut means "correct", however *mish mazbut* means "incorrect."

59

To remember	Yitzakkar
Your	Ilak, taba'ak
Number	Raqim/Ra'im
Hour	Sa'ah
Dark / darkness	Atma/ilatma
About / on the	An/ ala
Grandmother	Jiddah/Sit
Five	Khamsa
Minute / Minutes	Daqiqa/daqa'iq
More	Aktar
To think	Afakkir
School	Madrassah
To come	Aiji
To hear	Asma'
Last	Akhir

You need to remember my number
Inta mihtaj [or Lazim] titzakkar raqmi
This is the last hour of darkness
Hadi akhir sa'ah min il-atma
I want to come because I want to hear my grandmother speaking Arabic
Ana biddi aiji ashan asma' sitti btihki arabi
I need to think more about this, and what to do
Ana mihtaj afakkir fil ma'du'u aktar, wshu a'amil
From here to there, it's five minutes by car
Min hun lahinak masafit khamis daqayiq [Da'ayi'] fi sayara
The school on the mountain
Ilmadrassah ala iljabal

*The definition of *ma'du'u* is "topic," "matter," or "subject."

Early	Badri
To leave (a place)	Atrik/aruh
Again	Marra tanya
West Bank	Ildaffa ilgharbiyyah
To take	Akhud
To try	Iyjarrib
To rent	Yista'jir
Without her	Bidunha
We are	Nihna
To turn off	Atfi
To ask	As'al
To stop	Iywaqqif/iywa'if
Permission	Izin

He needs to leave and rent a house at the beach
Huwwa mihtaj yitrik wiyista'jir bait ala ilbahar
I want to take the test without her
Biddi Akhud ilfahis [ilimtihan] bidunha
We are here for a long time
Ihna hun min zaman
I need to turn off the lights early tonight
Mihtaj atfi ildaw badri illailah
We want to stop here
Bidna inwaqqif hun
We are from the West Bank
Nihna min ildaffa ilgharbiyyah
The same building
Ilimara nafsa
I want to ask permission to leave
Biddi ukhid izin atrik

*In Palestinian Arabic, the verb "to ask" can also be *akhud*, which means "to take."
*In Palestinian Arabic, the verb "to stop" is *twaqqif* or twa'if. However, "to cease" is *khalas*. For example, if someone is annoying you, you tell them, "Stop!" / *Khalas*!
*In Palestinian Arabic, the definition of "again" is *min kaman*. However, it can also be min *jedid* or *mara tenya*. All three can be used interchangeably.
*In Palestinian Arabic, the West Bank / *Ildaffa ilgharbiyyah* is usually pronounced as *ildaffa*.

To open	Aftah
A bit, a little, a little bit	Ishwayya
To pay	Adfa'a
Once again	Marra Tanya
There isn't/ there aren't	Mafish
Sister	Ukht
To hope	Yitmanna
To live (to exist)	A'ish
To live (in a place)	Askun
Nice to meet you	It-sha-rrafna
Name	Ism
Last name	Ism il'aila
To return	Arja'
Jerusalem	Alquds
Door	Bab

I need to open the door for my sister
Mihtaj [Biddi, or Lazim] aftah ilbab la ukhti

I need to buy something
Ana mihtaj ashtri shi

I want to meet your sisters
Ana biddi aqabil [a'abil] khawatak

Nice to meet you, what is your name and your last name
Itsharrafna bi ma'riftak, shu ismak wi'ism ailtak?

To hope for a little better
Batmanna shi ahsan shwai

I want to return from the United States and to live in Qatar without problems
Biddi arja' min Amirka wa askun fi Qatar bidun mashakil

I want to live 100 years
Biddi A'ish mit sana

I need to return your book
Lazim Arraji' lak ktabak

Why are you sad right now?
(M)Laish inta halqait [halla'] hazin? (F) Laish inti halqait hazina?

There isn't enough time to go to Jerusalem today
Mafish waqit [wa'it] kafi nruh ala Alquds ilyum

*In Palestinian Arabic, the definition of "nice to meet you" is *tsharafna, bima'riftak* for masculine cases, and *tsharafna bi ma'riftik* for feminine cases.

*This *isn't* a phrase book! The purpose of this book is *solely* to provide you with tools to create *your own* sentences!

To happen	Sa'ir/Huduth
To order	Talab/Amr
To drink	Shurub
Excuse me	La mu'akhaza / La ti akhizni
Child	(M)Walad, (F)bint
Woman	Mara
To begin / To start	Bidayat/ tablish
To finish	Takhlis
To help	Asa'id
To smoke	Adakkhin
To love	Hub
To talk / To Speak	Ahki / al-haki

This must happen today
Hada lazim ysir ilyum
Excuse me, my child is here as well
La mu'akhaza, ibni hun kaman
I love you
Bahibbak
I see you
Shayfak
I need you at my side
Mihtajak janbi
I need to begin soon because I need to finish before 3 o'clock in the afternoon
Lazim abda badri ashan akhallis qabil [Abil] ilsa'ah thalata ba'didduhur
I need help
Mihtaj musa'ada
I don't want to smoke once again
Ma biddi adakkhin tani marra
I want to learn to speak Arabic
Biddi At'allam al-haki bil arabi

*To help is *Yisa'id,* however "help!" is mus'ada
("I need help," "I need rescue" / *ana mihtaj il mus'ada*).

63

To read	Aqra or A'ra
To write	Aktab
To teach	Adarris
To close	Asakkir
To choose	Akhtar
To prefer	Afaddil
To put	Ahutt
Less	Aqal or A'al
Sun	Shams
Month	Shahar
I Talk	Bahki
Exact	Tamam/mazbut

I need this book to learn how to read and write in Arabic because I want to teach in Egypt
Mihtaj hada liktab ashan at'allam kif aqra wa aktab arabi, li'anni rah adarris fi Masir
I want to close the door of the house
Biddi Asakkir bab ilbait
I prefer to put the gift here
Bafaddil ahut ilhadiyah hawn
I want to pay less than you for the dinner
Biddi adfa'a aqal minnak ala il-asha
I speak with the boy and the girl in French
Ana bahki ma'a ilwalad wilbinit bil faransi
There is sun outside today
Ilyum, fi ishams barrah
Is it possible to know the exact date?
Mumkin a'arif iltarikh bilzabt?
I want to go to sleep now
Biddi rouh nam dilwati
Where is the airport?
Wain il-matar?

*With the knowledge you've gained so far, now try to create your own sentences!

To exchange (*money*)	Asruf
To call	Attisil
Brother	Akh
Dad	Baba
To sit	Aq'ud
Together	Ma'a ba'ad
To change	Yitghayyar
Of course	Taba'an
Welcome	Ahlan *or* Marhaba
During	Lamma *or* Wa'it
Years	Sana /Snii
Sky	Sama
Up	Fuq, Fu'u
Down	Tahit
Sorry	Asif
To follow	Yilhaq, Yilha
To the	Ila
Big	Kbir
New	Jdid
Never / ever	Abadan

I don't want to exchange the money at the bank
Ma biddi asruf liflus fil bank
I want to call my brother and my dad today
Biddi attisil fi akhuya wa abuya ilyum
Of course I can come to the theater, and I want to sit together with you and with your sister
Ta'ba'an ana baqdar aji alal cinema, wibiddi aq'ud ma'ak wa ma'a' ukhtak
I need to go down to see your new house
Lazim anzil tahit ashan ashuf baitak li-jdid
I can see the sky from the window
Baqdar ashuf ilsama min ilshubbak
I am sorry, but he wants to follow her to the store
Ana mit'assif, bas biddu yilhaqha ala ildukkan
I don't ever want to see you
Ma biddi ashufak abadan

*In Palestinian dialect, "brother" is *akh*, and "dad" is *baba*. However, "my dad" is *abuya*, and "my brother" is *akhuya*. "My sister" is *ukhti*, and "my mother" is *immi*.

*In the English language, the verb "to go down" isn't commonly used. However, in many foreign languages, the use of this verb is extremely prevalent.

To allow	Akhallih/ asmah
To believe	Asaddiq, asaddi'
Morning	Sabah
Except	Illa / Ma a'ada
To promise	Aw'id
Good night	Tisbah ala khair
To recognize	Yit'araf ala
People	Nas, Ashkhas, ahl
To move (an object)	Azih / Harrik
To move (to a place)	Yintiqil
Far	Ib'id
Different	Ghair
Man	Zalama
To enter	Yudkhul
To receive	Yistilim
Each, every	Kul
Good afternoon	Masa ilkhair
Left / right	Shmal/ Yamin
Him / Her	Huwwa/ Hiyya

I need to allow him to go with us
Lazim akhallih yruh ma'na
I believe everything except this
Basaddiq kulshi illa hada
I need to move the car because my sister needs to return home
Mihtaj Azih Ilsayyarah, li'n ukhti lazim tirja'a lalbait
I promise to say good night to my parents each night
Baw'id aqul [a'ul] tisbahu ala khair l'ahli kul laila
The people from Jordan are very pleasant
Ahl il urdun ktir latifin
I need to find another hotel very quickly
Mihtaj alaqi autail tani bisur'a
They need to receive a book for work
Mihtajin yistilmu ktab lal shughul
I see the sun in the morning
Bashuf ishams issubuh
The house is on the right end of the street
Il bait ala ilnahya ilyamin min ilshari'

*In Arabic, the article "the" is used when referring to countries, cities, or locations. "From Jordan" / *min il urdun.*

To wish	Atmanna
Bad	Atil/ mish mnih
To Get	Ajib
To forget	Ansa
Everybody / Everyone	Kulwahad/kulhada
Although	Ma' innu
To feel	Yihiss
Great	Azim
Next (following, after)	Jaya / Illi ba'du
To like	Ahib
In front	Quddam
Next (near, close)	Qarib/ Arib/ janb
Behind	Wara
Well	Ahsan
Goodbye	Awaddi
Restaurant	Mat'am
Bathroom	Hammam

I don't want to wish you anything bad
Ma biddi atmannalak shi atil
I must forget everybody from my past to feel relaxed
Lazim ansa kul illi irifithum fil madi ashan akun mirtah
I am next to the person behind you
Ana janb ilshakhs illi warak
There is a great person in front of me
Fi shakhis azim quddami
Where is the bathroom in the restaurant?
Wain ilhammam fil mata'am?
She has to get a car before the next year
Hiya lazim tjib sayarrah qabil issana iljaya
I like the house, but it is very small
Ajibni ilbait, lakinnu ktir sghir
Goodbye my friends
Bawaddi'as-habi

*The literal translation of *kul Illi irifthum* is "all those whom I knew."
*The literal translation of *akun mirtah* is "to be relaxed."

To remove / to take out	Yshil
Please	Ba'id iznak/min fadlak
Beautiful	(M)Hilo/(F)Hilwa
To lift	Arfa'a
Include / Including	Ma'
Belong	Mulk
To hold	Yimsik
To check	At'akkad
Small	Isghir
Real	Mazbut/haqiqi
Weather	Jaw
Size	Maqas/Hajim
High	A'li
Doesn't	Mish
So (as in then)	Yaani
So (as in very)	Ktir
Price	Si'ir

She wants to remove this door please
Hiyya bidha tshil hada ilbab min fadlak
This doesn't belong here, I need to check again
Hada mish lahun, lazim at'akkad marra tanya
This week the weather was very beautiful
Hada il-Usbu'u kan iljaw hilu ktir
I need to know which is the real diamond
Biddi A'arif, ayya fihum il almaza ilhaqiqiyyah
We need to see the size of the house
Mihtajin nshuf ish hajm ilbait
I want to lift this, so you need to raise it high
Biddi arfa' hada, ashan haik lazim tirfa'u ali
I can pay this even though that the price is so expensive
Baqdar adfa'a ma' innuh issi'ir ghali ktir

*In Palestinian Arabic, "beautiful" can be *hilu / hilwa*
or *jamil / jamila*. Both can be used interchangeably.
*The definition of *lahun* is "theirs."

BUILDING BRIDGES

In Building Bridges, we take six conjugated verbs that have been selected after studies I have conducted for several months in order to determine which verbs are most commonly conjugated into first person. For example, once you know how to say, "I need," "I want," "I can," and "I like," you will be able to connect words and say almost anything you want more correctly and understandably. The following three pages contain these six conjugated verbs in first, second, third, fourth, and fifth person, as well as some sample sentences. Please master the entire program up until here prior to venturing onto this section.

I want	Biddi
I need	Mihtaj
I can	Baqdar/Ba'dar
I like	Bahib
I go	Ana baruh
I have	Indi
I must / I have to	Ana lazim

I want to go to my house

Biddi aruh ala baiti

I can go with you to the bus station

Baqdar aruh ma'ak ala mahattit il-bas

I need to walk to the museum

Mihtaj amshi lal mat-haf

I like to take the train

Bahib akhud litrain [ilqitar]

I have a book

Indi ktab

I have to speak to my teacher

Lazim akallim ila mudarsi/ mudarristi [F]

Please master pages #47-#69, prior to attempting the following pages!!

You want / do you want - Inta biddak/ inta biddak?
He wants / does he want - Huwwa bidduh/ Bidduh huwwa?
She wants / does she want - Hiyya bidha/ Bidha hiyya?
We want / do we want - Bidna/ ihna bidna?
They want / do they want - Bidhum/ Hum bidhum?
You (plural) want? - Intu bidkum / Intu bidkum?

You need / do you need - Inta Mihtaj/Mihtaj inta?
He needs / does he need - Huwwa mihtaj/Mihtaj huwwa?
She needs / does she need - Hiyya mihtaja/ Mihtaja Hiyya?
We need / do we need - Ihna mihtajin/ Mihtajin ihna?
They need / do they need - Humma mihtajin/ Mihtajin humma?
You (plural) need? - Intu mihtajin/ Intu mihtajin? *Or* mihtajin intu?

You can / can you - Inta btiqdar/ Btiqdar inta?
He can / can he - Huwwa byiqdar/ Byiqdar huwwa?
She can / can she - Hiyya btiqdar/ Btiqdar hiyya?
We can / can we - Ihna bniqdar/ Bniqdar ihna?
They can / can they - Humma byiqdaru/byiqdaru humma or Humma byiqdaru?
You (plural) can? - Intu btiqdaru/ Btiqdaru intu? or intu btiqdaru?

You like / do you like - Inta bithib/ Bithib inta?
He likes / does he like - Huwwa biyhib/ Biyhib huwwa?
She like / does she like - Hiyya bithib/ bithib hiyya?
We like / do we like - Binhib/ binhib ihna?
They like / do they like - Humma biyhibbu/ Biyhibbu humma?
You (plura) like - Intu bithibbu

You go / do you go -Inta bitruh/ Bitruh inta?
He goes / does he go - Huwwa biyruh/ Biyruh huwwa?
She goes / does she go - Hiyya bitruh/ Bitruh hiyya?
We go / do we go - Ihna binruh/ Binruh ihna?
They go / do they go - Humma biyruhu/ Biyruhu humma?
You (plural) go - Ruhu intu

You have / do you have - Indak/ Fi indak?
He has / does he have - Indu/ Fi indu?
She has / does she have - Indha/ Fi indha?
We have / do we have - Indna/ Fi indna?
They have / do they have - Indhum/ Fi indhum?
You (plural) have - Indna

You must /must you? - Inta dururi [Lazim]/ Dururi [Lazim] inta?
He must/ must he? – Huwwa dururi/ Dururi huwwa?
She must/ must she – Hiyya dururi/ Dururi hiyya?
We must must we? – Ihna dururi/ Dururi ihna?
They must / must they? – Humma dururi/ Dururi humma?
You (plural) must - Intu dururi/ Dururi into?

Do you want to go?
Biddak truh?
Does he want to fly?
Biddu ytir?
We want to swim
Bidna nisbah
Do they want to run?
Bidhum Yurkudu?
Do you need to clean?
Mihtaj tnadif?
She needs to sing a song
Hiyya mihtaja tghani ughniya
We need to travel
Ihna mihtajin nsafir
They don't need to fight
Humma mish mihtajin yitkhanaqu
You (plural) need to see
Intu mihtajin tshufu
Can you hear me?
Qadir [or Ader] tisma'ni?
Yes, he can dance very well
Sahih, huwwa byiqdar yurqus mnih
We can go out tonight
Bniqdar nitla'a illaila
They can break the wood
Humma Byiqdaru yikasru il-khashab
Do you like to eat here?
Bithib tukil han [or hawn]?

He likes to spend time here
Huwwa biyhib yqaddi waqt han
[or hawn]
We like to fix the house
Ihna binhib nsallih ilbait
They like to cook
Humma biyhibbu yutbukhu
You (plural) like my house
Intu bithibbu baiti
Do you go to school today?
Rayih [F:Rayha] ala il madrassa
ilyum?
He goes fishing
Huwwa biyruh ysid samak
We are going to relax
Ihna rah nrayyih
They go to watch a film
Humma biyruhu yihdaru filim
Do you have money?
Indak masari?
She must look outside
Hiyya daruri [or Lazim] tittala'a
barra
We have to sign our names
Ihna lazim nwaqqi'I isimna
They have to send the letter
Lazim yib'atu il maktub
You (plural) have to order
Intu lazim tutlubu [or tsawwu
talabiyyah]

Countries of the Middle East
Dual al-sharq al-aa'ou'satt

Lebanon	Libnan
Syria	Surya
Jordan	Il-urdun
Israel/Palestine/West Bank	Isra'il/ Falastin/ Iddiffah il-Gharbiyyah
Iraq	Il-Iraq
Saudi Arabia	Il-Suudiyah
Kuwait	Likwait
Qatar	Qatar
Bahrain	Il-Bahrain
United Arab Emirates	Il-Imarat
Oman	Uman
Yemen	Il-Yaman
Egypt	Masir
Libya	Libya
Tunisia	Tunis
Algeria	Aljez-har
Morocco	Il-Maghrib

Months

January	Kanun ittani
February	Shbat
March	Adhar
April	Nisan
May	Ayyar
June	Hziran
July	Tammuz
August	Ab
September	Aylul
October	Tishrin il-Awwal
November	Tishrin ittani
December	Kanun Il-Awwal

Days of the Week

Sunday	Il-Ahad
Monday	Litnain
Tuesday	Il-Talata
Wednesday	Il-Arba'a
Thursday	Il-Khamis
Friday	Il-Jum'a
Saturday	Il-Sabit

Seasons

Spring	Il-Rabi'i
Summer	Il-Saif
Autumn	Il-Kharif
Winter	Il-shita

Cardinal Directions

North	Shmal
South	Junub
East	Sharq
West	Gharb

Colors

Black	(M)Aswad (F)Sauda
White	(M)Abyad (F)Baida
Gray	(M)Sakani/ramadi (F)Sakaniyyah/Ramadiyya
Red	(M)Ahmar (F)Hamra
Blue	(M)Azraq (F)Zarqa
Yellow	(M)Asfar (F)Safra
Green	(M)Akhdar (F)Khadra
Orange	(M) Burtqani (F)Burtqaniyya
Purple	Lailaki
Brown	(M)Binni (F)Binniyya

Numbers

One	Wahad	**Twenty**	Ishrin
Two	Itnain	**Thirty**	Talatin
Three	Talata	**Forty**	Arb'in
Four	Arba'a	**Fifty**	Khamsin
Five	Khamsa	**Sixty**	Sittin
Six	Sitta	**Seventy**	Sab'in
Seven	Sab'a	**Eighty**	Tamanin
Eight	Tamanya	**Ninety**	Tis'in
Nine	Tis'a	**Hundred**	Miyya
Ten	Ashara	**Thousand**	Alif
		Million	Malyun

Conversational
Arabic
Quick and Easy

YATIR NITZANY

SYRIAN ARABIC DIALECT

The Levant is a historical, broad geographic region of the eastern Mediterranean that includes Cyprus, Jordan, Lebanon, Palestine, Israel, and Syria. Arabic speakers in this area have their own distinctive dialect of Modern Standard Arabic, Levantine Arabic, also referred to as Mediterranean Arabic, which is closer to Egyptian Arabic than it is to Gulf Arabic. The people of the Levant share not only a long history, but also similar cuisines and customs, and Levantine Arabic is but one more example of the widespread commonalities linking the peoples and nations of the region. Though Levantine Arabic is not the official language of any country, it is commonly spoken throughout the region by more than twenty million speakers in the Levant alone, and millions more across the globe, making it one of the most extensively spoken dialects of the eastern Mediterranean. The dialect is spoken and does not have a set written form. While spoken Levantine Arabic retains many of the features of other forms of Arabic, some differences exist, and a thorough knowledge of these differences is essential to becoming conversational in Levantine Arabic. Levantine Arabic itself is broken down into a variety of subdialects with their own special differences and idiosyncrasies, including Lebanese, Jordanian, Palestinian, and Syrian, and we'll be exploring the Syrian dialect of Levantine Arabic in this course.

Spoken in: Syria

MEMORIZATION MADE EASY

There is no doubt the three hundred and fifty words in my program are the required essentials in order to engage in quick and easy basic conversation in any foreign language. However, some people may experience difficulty in the memorization. For this reason, I created Memorization Made Easy. This memorization technique will make this program so simple and fun that it's unbelievable! I have spread the words over the following twenty pages. Each page contains a vocabulary table of ten to fifteen words. Below every vocabulary box, sentences are composed from the words on the page that you have just studied. This aids greatly in memorization. Once you succeed in memorizing the first page, then proceed to the second page. Upon completion of the second page, go back to the first and review. Then proceed to the third page. After memorizing the third, go back to the first and second and repeat. And so on. As you continue, begin to combine words and create your own sentences in your head. Every time you proceed to the following page, you will notice words from the previous pages will be present in those simple sentences as well, because repetition is one of the most crucial aspects in learning any foreign language. Upon completion of your twenty pages, *congratulations*, you have absorbed the required words and gained a basic, quick-and-easy proficiency and you should now be able to create your own sentences and say anything you wish in the Arabic language. This is a crash course in conversational Syrian dialect, and it works!

ARABIC PRONUNCIATIONS

PLEASE MASTER THE FOLLOWING PAGE IN ARABIC PRONUNCIATIONS PRIOR TO STARTING THE PROGRAM

Kha . For Middle Eastern languages including Arabic, Hebrew, Farsi, Pashto, Urdu, Hindi, etc., and also German, to properly pronounce the kh or ch is essential, for example, *Khaled* (a Muslim name) or *Chanukah* (a Jewish holiday) or *Nacht* ("night" in German). The best way to describe kh or ch is to say "ka" or "ha" while at the same time putting your tongue at the back of your throat and blowing air. It's pronounced similarly to the sound that you make when clearing your throat. Please remember this whenever you come across any word containing a kh in this program.

Ghayin . The Arabic *gh* is equivalent to the "g" in English, but its pronunciation more closely resembles the French "r," rather than "g." Pronounce it at the back of your throat. The sound is equivalent to what you would make when gargling water. Gha is pronounced more as "rha," rather than as "ga." *Ghada* is pronounced as "rhada." In this program, the symbol for ghayin is gh, so keep your eyes peeled.

Aayin is pronounced as *a'a*, pronounced deep at the back of your throat. Rather similar to the sound one would make when gagging. In the program, the symbol for *aayin* is *a'a, u'u, o'o,* or *i'i.*

Ha is pronounced as "ha." Pronunciation takes place deep at the back of your throat, and for correct pronunciation, one must constrict the back of the throat and exhale air while simultaneously saying "ha." In the program, this strong h ("ha") is emphasized whenever *ha, ah, hi, he,* or *hu* is encountered.

NOTE TO THE READER

The purpose of this book is merely to enable you to communicate in Syrian Arabic. In the program itself (pages 17-39) you may notice that the composition of some of those sentences might sound rather clumsy. This is intentional. These sentences were formulated in a specific way to serve two purposes: to facilitate the easy memorization of the vocabulary and to teach you how to combine the words in order to form your own sentences for quick and easy communication, rather than making complete literal sense in the English language. So keep in mind that this is not a phrase book!

As the title suggests, the sole purpose of this program is for conversational use only. It is based on the mirror translation technique. These sentences, as well as the translations are not incorrect, just a little clumsy. Latin languages, Semitic languages, and Anglo-Germanic languages, as well as a few others, are compatible with the mirror translation technique.

Many users say that this method surpasses any other known language learning technique that is currently out there on the market. Just stick with the program and you will achieve wonders!

Again, I wish to stress this program is by no means, shape, or form a phrase book! The sole purpose of this book is to give you a fundamental platform to enable you to connect certain words to become conversational. Please also read the "Introduction" and the "About Me" section prior to commencing the program.

In order to succeed with my method, please start on the very first page of the program and fully master one page at a time prior to proceeding to the next. Otherwise, you will overwhelm yourself and fail. Please do not skip pages, nor start from the middle of the book.

It is a myth that certain people are born with the talent to learn a language, and this book disproves that myth. With this method, anyone can learn a foreign language as long as he or she follows these explicit directions:

* Memorize the vocabulary on each page

* Follow that memorization by using a notecard to cover the words you have just memorized and test yourself.

* Then read the sentences following that are created from the vocabulary bank that you just mastered.

* Once fully memorized, give yourself the green light to proceed to the next page.

Again, if you proceed to the following page without mastering the previous, you are guaranteed to gain nothing from this book. If you follow the prescribed steps, you will realize just how effective and simplistic this method is.

THE PROGRAM

Let's Begin! "Vocabulary" (Memorize the Vocabulary)

I	I am	Ana
With you	(Masculine) Ma'ak / (Fem) ma'aik
With him / with her	Ma'au / ma'aa
With us	Ma'ana
For you	(Masc) Ilak / (Fem) Ilik
Without him	Bidunu
Without them	Bidunun
Always	Dayman
Was	Kan
This, This is	(Masc) had / (Fem) hay
Today	Alyoum
Sometimes	Ahyanan
Maybe	Yumkin , Bjouz
Are you?	(M)Inte?, (F)Inti?
Better	Ahsan, Afdal
You, you are	(M)Inte / (F)inti
He / She	Huwwe/Hiyye
From	Min

Sentences from the vocabulary (now you can speak the sentences and connect the words)

I am with you
Ana ma'ak
This is for you
(Masc) Hada Ilak
(Fem) Hada Ilik
I am from Dubai
Ana min Dubai
Are you from Syria?
(Masc) Inte min Sourya?
(Fem) Inti min Sourya

Sometimes you are with us at the mall
(Masc) Ahyanan betakun "Inte" ma'ana bel soua' (mol) / (Fem) Ahyanan betkouni "Inti" Ma'ana bel soua'
I am always with her
Ana dayman ma'aa
Are you without them today?
(Masc) Alyoum inte bidunun?
Sometimes I am with him
Ahyanan bkoun ma'ahu
(Fem) alyoum inti bedounun?

*In Classic Arabic, there are gender rules. The masculine case for "for you" is *laka*; the feminine case is *laki*. The endings of *ka* and *ki* are used quite often in the Arabic language to signify gender. However in the Damascus dialect, it is a little bit different. The masculine case for "for you" is *ilak*; the feminine case is *ilik*. The endings of *ak* and *ik* are used quite often in the Syrian Arabic to signify gender.

I was	Ana kent
To be	(M)Ykun / (F) Tkun
The	Al/el
Same / like *(as in similar)*	Nafs / mitil
Good	Mnih/kwayyes
Here	Hon
Very	Kteer
And	Wa
Between	Beyn
Now	Halla'
Later / After / afterwards	Ba'adeyn
If	Iza
Yes	Eyh
To No	La'
Tomorrow	Bukra
Person	Shakhs / Flan
Also / too / as well	Kaman

It's better tomorrow
Bukra Ahsan

This is good as well
Kaman Had Mnih

To be the same person
Beykoun nafs el shakhs

Yes, you are very good
Eyh , Inte kteer mnih

I was here with them
Kent "ana" hon ma'aun

You and I
Ana we Inte

The same day
Nafs alyom

*In this program, the article "the" *al* will sometimes become a prefix at the beginning of the noun or become suffix at the end of the proposition. For nouns beginning with *d, n, r, s, sh, t, th,* and *z* the *l* is omitted and replaced with the initial consonant of the following noun. "The people" / *al-shakhs* is *ashakhs.* "The Nile" / *al-nil* is *an-nil.* It is dropped when spoken; however, when written, it's usually *al-shaks* or *al-nil.*
*The words between the symbols "¬ " are optional. It is understood with or without those words because of the verb endings—conjugation.
Betkoun/betkouni/beykoun means "to be." We add "be" when conjugating.
*In Syrian dialect *shakhs* is used to signify a "person," however *flan* is used to signify an unknown person.

Me	Ni /-i
Ok	Tamam
Even if	Hatta iza
No	La'
Worse	Aswa'
Where	Weyn
Everything	Kel shi
Somewhere	Bshi makan
What	Shou
Almost	Ta'riban
There	Hnik
I go	"Ana" brouh

Afterwards is worse
Elli jaye aswa'
Even if I go now
Hatta iza reht "ana" halla'
Where is everything?
Weyn kel shi?
Maybe somewhere
Yemkun bshi mkan
What? I am almost there
shou? Ana ta'riban wselet
Where are you?
Weynak?
Where is the hospital
Weyn el mashfa?

*The translation of the sentence "Afterwards is worse." / *Elli jaye aswa'* means literally "the coming worse" (or "what is coming is worse").
*The translation of the sentence "What? I am almost there." / *Shou*? *Ana ta'riban wselet,* literally means "What? I have almost arrived." The word "there" cannot be translated literally in this sentence and is not spoken in the Damascus dialect.
Fi makan literally means in a place.
*In Damascus dialect the pronoun me has several forms, when it comes as direct object it comes as a suffix "ni" at the end of the verb. For example "Help me" is *saa'edni* and when it comes as indirect object comes as a suffix *li* at the end of the verb. For example "Tell me" *illi*. The indirect object is the receiver of the action or the receiver of the result of an action. "Bring her" (direct) *jiba* / (indirect) *jibla*. "Bring him" (direct) *jibu* / (indirect) *jiblu*. "Bring them" (direct) *jibun* / (indirect) *jiblun*. "Bring us" (direct) *jibna* / (indirect) *jiblna*.

House	Beyt
In, at, at the	Fi /bel- /be-
Car	Sayyarah
Already	Al-An
Good morning	Sabah el-kheyr
How are you?	(M)kifak?/ (F)kifek?
Where are you from?	(M)Min weyn Inte?(F)Min weyn Inti
Impossible	Mustahil
Hello	Marhaba
What is your name?	(M) Shou Ismak? / (F) Shou ismik?
How old are you?	(M) Adeysh Umrak? / (F) Adeysh Umrek?
Son	Ibn
Daughter	Bent
To have	A'andi
Doesn't *or* **isn't**	(M)(F)(for adjectives) Mo / (for verbs) Ma
Hard	Sa'ab
Still	Lessa

She doesn't have a car, so maybe she is still at the house
"Heyye" ma A'anda sayyarah, fa yemkin lessata bel beyt
I am in the car with your son and daughter
(M) Ana besayyarah Ma'aa Ibnak we bentak
(F)Ana besayyarah Ma'aa Ibnek we bentek
Good morning, how are you today?
Saba el-kheyr, Kefak(M)/Kefek(F) alyom?
Hello, what is your name?
Marhaba, Shou ismak?
How old are you?
Adeysh Umrak?
This is very hard, but it's not impossible
(M) Had kteer sa'ab, bas mo mustahil (F) Hay kteer sa'abe, bas mo mustahila
Where are you from?
Min weyn inte?

*In Arabic, possessive pronouns become suffixes to the noun. For example, for the English word "your," *ka* is the masculine form, and *ki* feminine form.
-"Your book" / *ktabaka* (m.), *ktabiki* (f.)
-"Your house" / *manzilika* (m.), *manziliki* (f.)
*In Damascus dialect, possessive pronouns become suffixes to the noun. For example, for the English word "your," *ak* is the masculine form, and *ek* feminine form. "Your book": *ketabak* (M) / *ketabek* (F)
*In the Arabic language, as well as in other Semitic languages, the article "a" doesn't exist. " for example she doesn't have a car" / *hiyya ma a'anda sayyarah.*
*In the Damascus dialect, the endings of certain adjectives vary depending on the gender and on whether it is singular or plural. For example, "a nice car" / *Sayyarah helwe.* The car is feminine; the adjective ending contains an "e." However the endings of masculine adjectives remain the same, for example, "your son is clever" / *Ibnak zaki.* In the plural case, the adjective usually ends with an "e," for example, "nice books" / *keteb helwe,* and of course, there are exceptions.

Thank you	Shukran/ yeslamo
For	Meshan/menshan
Anything	Ayya shi
That, That is	(M) Hadak/ (F) Hadik
Time	Wa't
But	Bas
No/ Not	La'/ mo, ma
I am not	Ana mo / ana ma
Away	Ba'aid
Late	Meta'akhir
Similar, like	Byetshab / byeshbah
Another/ Other	Shi tani/hada tani
Side	Janib, taraf
Until	La / laa'and
Yesterday	Embareh
Without us	Bedunna
Since	Min lamma/min
Day	Yom
Before	A'bl

Thanks for anything
Shukran ala Ayya Shi
I am not here, I am away
And mo hon, ana bmkan tani
That is a similar house
Had beyt byshbah……
I am from the other side
And min eltarf eltani
But I was here until late yesterday
Bas ana kent hon embareh la wa'et meta'kher
I am not at the other house
And mo bel beyt el tani

*In Arabic there are 3 definitions for time:
-Time, *wai't* refers to; era, moment period, duration of time.
-Time(s), *marra(t)* refers to; occasion or frequency.
-Time, *sa'a* in reference to; hour, what time is it.
**Makan akhar* literally means "another place."
*We say, "I am not," based on the word after it. For example, if it is an adjective or noun, we use *mo*, and if it is a verb, we use *ma*.

I say / I am saying	Ana ba'uol
What time is it?	Adeysh essa'a?
I want	Ana biddi
Without you	(M) Bidounak / (F) bidounik
Everywhere /wherever	Bkil mkan/ b ay makan
I am going	(M) ana rayeh /(F)ana rayha
With	Ma'a
My	Ili
Cousin	(M)Ibn il'am (or) Ibn ilkhal [uncle from mother's side), (P) wlad al'am / wlad alkhal (F)Bent al'am/ Bent alkhal, (P)banat al'am, banat alkhal
I need	"Ana" ahtaj / lazim
Right now	Halla' / bhay ellahza
Night	Leyl/ masa
To see	Shouf
Light	Dhau
Outside	Barra
Without	Bidoun/bala
Happy	Farhan/mabsout
I see / I am seeing	Ana Bshouf

I am saying no / I say no
Ana ba'oul la'
I want to see this today
(M) Biddi Shoufo alyom/(F) biddi shoufa alyom
I am with you everywhere
Ana ma'aka fi kulli makan
I am happy without my cousins here
(M)"Ana" mabsout bedoun wlad Ammi hon
(F) "Ana" mabsouta bedoun wlad Ammi hon
I need to be there at night
Lazim koun hnek belleyl
I am seeing light outside
A'am shouf dhau barra
What time is it right now?
Adeysh essa'a halla'?

*My is a possessive pronoun that comes as a suffix to a noun (i) in Syrian dialect. For example, "father" is *ab* while "my father" is *abi*. "Cup" is *koob* while "my cup" is *koobi*. For second and third person, "Your father" is *abook* if masculine, and *abooki* if feminine. "Your father" is *abookon* if masculine/ feminine plural. "His father" is *aboo*. "Her Father" is *abowa/aboha*. "Their Father" is (abowwon) if masculine & feminine. "Our Father" is *abona*. "Your car" / *sayartak*. (M)(F) "Your (plural) car" / *sayartakun*. "His car"/ *sayartu*. "Her car" / *sayarta*. "Our car" / *sayartnaa*. (M)(F) "Their car" / *sayart'hun*.
*This isn't a phrase book! The purpose of this book is solely to provide you with the tools to create your own sentences!

Place	Makan
Easy	Sahel
To find	La'i
To look for/to search	Ydawwer
Near / Close	A'rib
To wait	Ystanna
To sell	Ybia'a
To use	Yesta'amil
To know	Ya'aref
To decide	Ya'rir
Between	Beyn
Next to	Janb
To	A'al / Lil- "prefix"

This place is easy to find
Had al makan sahel tlaa'i
I want to look for this next to the car
Biddi dawwer janb elsayyarah
I am saying to wait until tomorrow
Ana ba'oul nestanna la bukra
This table is easy to sell
Hay ettawleh beshoule btnbaa'a
I want to use this
Biddi ista'amil had/hay
I need to know where is the house
Lazim aa'aref weyn elbeyt
I want to decide between both places
Biddi a'rir beyn makanen

*Verbs conjugating: present tense
When there is more than one verb, we conjugate the first verb in the normal way and the second verb in a different way, and when it comes after the negation. From the first example above:
"I want to answer many questions" / *Biddi jaweb ala asa'lla kteer*
With the verb "answer" / *jaweb*, we see here that *jaweb* is not conjugated in the normal way.
 The conjugation of the second verb is:
"I answer" / *jaweb* = stem
"He answers / *yjaweb* = y + stem
She answers / *tjaweb* = t + stem
They answer / *yjawebun* = y + stem + *un*
You answer(M) / *tjaweb* = t + stem
You answer(F) / *tjawebi* = t + stem + *i*
We answer / *njaweb* = n + stem
You answer (plural) / *tjawbun* = t + stem + *un*. (The vowel is dropped.)

Because	La'innu
To buy	Yeshteri
Life	Hayah
Them, They	Henne
Bottle	Anine
Book	Ktab
Mine	Ili
To understand	Yafham
Problem / Problems	Meshkleh/ mashakel
I do / I am doing	A'am ea'amil
Of	Min
To look	Shouf
Myself	Nafsi
Enough	Ykaffi/kafi
Food / water	Akl/ May
Each/ every/ entire/ all	Kel/ kel/ kel/kel
Hotel	Fundua' /Otel

I like this hotel because I want to look at the beach
Ana bheb had el otel la'innu biddi shouf el shatia'
I want to buy a bottle of water
Biddi ishteri anninet may
I do this every day
Ana ba'amil hek kel yom
Both of them have enough food
Hinne letnen Andon akel beykaffi
That is the book, and that book is mine
Had hewwe el ktab, we had el ktab ili
I need to understand the problem
Lazim ifham el meshkleh
I see the view of the city from the hotel
Am shouf manzar el madina mn el otel
I do my homework today
Rah ia'amil wazifti elyom
My entire life/ all my life
Kel Hayati

*Sometimes the vowels are dropped in verbs or prepositions, for example, "from the house" / *mn el beyt.*

I like	Bheb
There is / There are	Fi
Family / Parents	A'ayle/ Ahl
Why	Leysh
To say	Y'oul
Something	Shai
To go	Yrouh
Ready	Jahiz
Soon	A'rib
To work	Yshtighil
Who	Miin
Busy	Mashgul
That (conjunction)	Innu
I Must	Lazim
Important	Muhim / dharouri

I like to be at my house with my parents
Bheb koun belbeyt ma'aa ahli
I want to know why I need to say something important
Biddi a'a'arif leysh lazim ihki shi Muhim
I am there with her
Ana hniik ma'aa
I am busy, but I need to be ready soon
Ana mashghoul, bas lazim koun jahiz A'an a'rib
I like to go to work
Bheb rouh a'al shighil
Who is there?
Miin hon?
I want to know if they are here, because I want to go outside
Biddi A'a'arif iza henne hon, la'innu biddi itla'a "rouh barra"
There are seven dolls
Fi saba'a ala'aab
I need to know that that is a good idea
Biddi A'a'arif innu hay fikra mniha

*In the last sentence, we use "that" as a conjunction (innu) as well as a demonstrative pronoun (had / hay).
*In some cases, in order to use "soon," we need to put a preposition before it—
A'an—as in the example above.

How much /How many	Adeysh?
To bring	Yjeeb
With me	Ma'ai
Instead	Badal
Only	Bas
When	Lamma
I can / Can I?	Fini / ya'dir
Or	Aw / wella
Were	Kan
Without me	Beduni
Fast	Sari' / bsera'a
Slow	Bati' / Bbeta'a
Cold	Barid
Inside	Juwwat / be-
To eat	Yakul
Hot	Har / harara
To Drive	Ysoua'

How much money do I need to bring with me?
Adeysh masari lazim jeeb ma'ai?
Instead of this cake, I want that cake
Badal hay el keka, biddi hay el keka
Only when you can
Bas lamma btea'dirThey were without me yesterday
Kanu embareh bedouni
Do I need to drive the car fast or slow?
Lazim souqa' essayyarah bsera'a wella bbeta'a
It is cold inside the library
Barda belmaktaba
Yes, I like to eat this hot for my lunch
Eyh, bheb bakul el ghada bhay el harara
I can work today
Ma fini ishtighil elyom

*"Were, *kan*, but for "they were," add the suffix to the pronoun: *kanu*.
"We were" is *kunna*.

To answer	Yjaweb
To fly	Yteer
Time / Times	Marra / Marrat
To travel	Ysafer
To learn	Yta'allam
How	Keef
To swim	Ysbah
To practice	Ytrrab
To play	Yla'aab
To leave (something)	Ytrek
Many /much /a lot	Kteer
I go to	Ana brouh le
First	Awwal
Time / Times	Marra/marrat
Around	Hawl

I want to answer many questions
Biddi jaweb ala asa'lla kteer
I must travel to Syria today
Lazim safer elyom a'suryia
I need to learn to swim at the pool
Lazim ita'allam essebaha bel masbah
I want to learn to play better tennis
Biddi ita'allam ala'ab tennis ahsan
I want to leave this here for you when I go to travel the world
Biddi itriklak el makan lamma safer bel a'alam
Since the first time
Min elmarra alawla
The children are yours
Al wlad ilak

*In Arabic; to leave (something) is *tark*.
To leave (a place) is *mughadarat*.
*In Arabic there are 3 definitions for time:
-Time, *wai't* refers to; era, moment period, duration of time.
-Time(s), *marra(t)* refers to; occasion or frequency.
-Time, *sa'a* in reference to; hour, what time is it.
Bishaklin literally means in a manner, in a form.
*With the knowledge you've gained so far, now try to create
your own sentences!

Nobody / Anyone	Ma hada / ay hada
Against	Dhid
Us	Nehnne
To visit	Yzour
Mom / Mother	Mama, um
To give	Ya'ati
Which	Ay
To meet	Ylta'i
Someone	Hada
Just	Bas
To walk	Ymshi
Week	Isbua'a / jema'a
Towards	Bi ittijah
Than	Min
Nothing	Wala shi

Something is better than nothing
Shi ahsan min wala shi

I am against her
Ana dhidda

We go to visit my family each week
Menrouh nzour a'aylti kel isbua'a

I need to give you something
Lazim aa'atik shi

Do you want to go meet someone?
Biddak trouh tlta'i hada?

I was here on Wednesdays as well
Kent hon ayyam el-arbia'aa' kaman

Do you do this everyday?
Bta'amil had/hay kel yom?

*In Damascus dialect when using the pronoun "You" as a suffix—*ak* or
lak if masculine, *ik* or *lik* if feminine, it is actually used as a direct and indirect
object pronoun (the person who is actually affected by the action which is
being carried out) in relation to a verb, the pronoun you becomes a suffix to
that verb, "I Love You" is *bhebbak* if masculine & *bhebbik* if feminine. "I Tell
you" is *be'illak* if masculine & *be'illik* if feminine. For a third person "I Tell
You" is *be'ilkon* if masculine or feminine plural.

I have	A'andi
Don't	Ma
Friend	Sadia'/sahib/rfeea'
To borrow	Ystaa'air
To look like / resemble	Yshbah
Grandfather	Jed
To want	Yrid / bid-
To stay	Ydhal
To continue	Ykammil
Way (road, path)	Tariq
Way (method)	Taria'a
I dont	Ana ma
To show	Yshawwef
To prepare	Yhaddir
I am not going	Ana mali rayeh

Do you want to look like Salim?
Biddak tseer tshbah salim? *(do you want to become to look like salim?")*
I want to borrow this book for my grandfather
Biddi astaa'air had el ktab meshan jeddi
I want to drive and to continue on this way to my house
Biddi soua' we kammel bhad el taria' labeyti
This isn't the way to do this
Mo hek ta'mla
I have a friend there, that's why I want to stay in Damascus
A'adi rfeea' hnik, lahashi biddi dhal bel dimashq
I am not going to see anyone here
Ma rah shouf had hon
I need to show you how to prepare breakfast
Biddi shawfak keyf t-hadder el ftour
Why don't you have the book?
Leysh ma andak el ktab?
That is incorrect, I don't need the car today
Had mo sahih, mali bhajet el sayyarah elyom

*Sahih means "correct"; however, mo sahih means "incorrect."
*Lahashi means "that's why."
*In Damascus Arabic, "I am going to" / rah means exactly the same, and it's in the future
 tense too.
*T-h pronounced normally one after the other, "t" followed by "h." The symbol - was
 inserted to clarify that it is not the same as "th" in English.
*The definition of "to ask" is Ysa'al (for questions) / Yutlub (to demand).
*To signify "while," we can either use fatra or zaman. However, fatra is used in the
 context of "during," while zaman is used in the context of time.
*Mali signifies "am not," for example, "I don't need" is translated and used as mali bhajet,
 which means literally "am not in need." Ana mali rayeh / "am not going."
 means "like this."

To remember	Ytzakkar
Your	Ilak
Number	Ra'm
Hour	Sa'ah
Dark / darkness	A'tme / dhalma
About / on the	A'al/be-
Grandmother	Sett
Five	Khamse
Minute / Minutes	Da'ia'a/Da'ayea'
More	Aktar
To think	Yfakker
To do	Ya'mel
To come	Yiji
To hear	Ysma'a
Last	Akhir
To talk / To Speak	Yihki

You need to remember my number
Lazim tetzakkar ra'mi
This is the last hour of darkness
Hay Akhir sa'ah dhalma/a'tma
I want to come to hear my grandmother speak Arabic
Biddi iji isma'a setti tehki a'arabi
I need to think more about this, and what to do
Lazim fakker belmawdoua'a aktar, we a'arif shou biddi a'amel
From here to there, it's only five minutes
Min hon la hnik, khams da'ayea' bas
The school on the mountain
El madraseh A'al jabal

*The definition of *mawdoua'a'* is "topic," "subject," "matter."
*In Arabic, nouns ending with an "a" or "ah" are feminine, those ending with a consonant are male. "The car" / *sayyarah* is feminine, "the book" / *al katab* is male.
—When pertaining to a demonstrative pronoun, the word "is" is translated as (M)*hay*/(F)*had*, for example, "That is incorrect" *Had mo sahih* or "That is a good idea" *hay fikra mniha*.
—When pertaining to a noun, for example, "is it?" the word "is" can refer to either a masculine or feminine noun. However, whenever pertaining to a masculine or feminine noun, it will become *howa* or *heyaa*. For example, when referring to a feminine noun such as *sayaara* / "the car," "is it (the car in question) here?" / *Heyaa hon?* When referring to a masculine noun such as *kaleb* / "a (male) dog," "is it (the dog in question) on the table?" / *hewwe a'al maida?*
-However, I yet again wish to stress that this isn't a grammar book!

Early	Bakkiir
To leave (to go)	Ytla'a/yrouh
Again	Marra tanye
Arabic	Arabi
To take	Yakhud
To try	Yhawel
To rent	Ysta'jir
Without her	Biduniha
We are	Nehne
To turn off	Ytfi/Ytaffi
To ask	Ysa'al//Yutlub
To stop	Yoa'af
Permission	Izin
While	Fatra/zaman

He needs to leave and rent a house at the beach
Biddu ytla'a we ysta'jir beyt a'al shatia'
We are here a long while
Nehne hon min zaman
I need to turn off the lights early tonight
Lazim itfi el adhwye bakkiir elmasa
We want to stop here
Bidna noa'af hon
We are from the Middle East
Nehne mn el sharia' alawsat
The same building
Nafs el benaa'
I want to ask permission to leave
Biddi utlub izin mshan rouh

*The definition of *to ask* is Ysa'al(for questions)/Yutlub (to demand).
*To signify *while* we can either use fatra or zaman. However *fatra* is used in the context of *during* while *zaman* is used in the the context of *time*.
*Mshan means "in order to."

95

To open	Yiftah
A bit, a little, a little bit	Shway
To pay	Yidfa'a
Once again	Marra tanye
There isn't/ there aren't	Ma fi
Sister	Ikhit
To hope	Yitmanna
To live (to exist)	Ya'ish
To live (in a place)	Yuskun
Nice to meet you	Tsharrafet bma'ariftak
Name	Isim
Last name	Kenye
To return	Yerjja'a
Aleppo / Palmyra	Haleb / Tadmur
Door	Bab

I need to open the door for my sister
Lazim iftah el bab la ikhti

I need to buy something
Lazim istiri shi

I want to meet your sisters
Biddi iltia'I ikhwatak

Nice to meet you, what is your name and your last name
Tsharrafet bma'ariftak, shou ismak we kenyetak?

I want to return to Aleppo
Biddi irja'a a'ala haleb

I want to live 100 years
Biddi 'ish 100 sene

I need to return your book
Lazim rajjea' ktabak

Why are you sad right now?
(M)leysh za'alan halla'? (F) leysh za'alana halla'?

There aren't any people here
Mafi ay hada hon

There isn't enough time to go to Palmyra today
Ma fi waa't el yom mshan el rouha A'l tadmur

*This isn't a phrase book! The purpose of this book is solely to provide you with the tools to create your own sentences!

To happen	Ysiir
To order	Yatlub
To drink	Yshrab
Excuse me	A'n iznak/Ba'd iznak
Child	(M)Walad, (F)binet
Woman	Mara
To begin / To start	Yibda'
To finish	Ykhallis
To help	Ysa'id
To smoke	Ydakhin
To love	Yheb
Afternoon	Ba'da el-dheher

This must happen today
Had lazim ysiir el yom
Excuse me, my child is here with me as well
A'n iznak, Ibni ma'I mon kaman
I love you
(M) bhebbak /(F) behebbik
I see you
bshoufak
I need you at my side
Mehtajak bjanbi
I need to begin soon in order to finish at 3 o'clock in the afternoon
Lazim ballish a'n a'riib mshan khallis essa'a 3 ba'd eldheher
I need help
Lazmni msaa'ade
I don't want to smoke once again
Ma a'ad biddi dakhin mara tanye
I want to learn how to speak Arabic
Biddi ita'allam ihki a'rabi

*To help is *asa'id,* however "help!" is *mus'ada* (I need help, I need rescue / *ana mihtaj la mus'ada*).

To read	Yia'ra
To write	Yiktib
To teach	Yita'allam
To close	Ysakker
To choose	Yikhtar
To prefer	Yfadhil
To put	Yhit
Less	Aa'al
Sun	Shames
Month	Shaher
I Talk	Ana ihki
Exact	Bezzabt

I need this book to learn how to read and write in the Arabic language because I want to study in Egypt
Lazmni had el ktab mshan ita'allam keyf Ia'ara we uktub bel a'arabi, la'innu biddi idrus b maser
I want to close the door of the house
Biddi sakker bab el beyt
I prefer to put the gift here
Bfadhil hit el hadiyye hon
I want to pay less than you for the dinner
Biddi idfaa' aa'al minnak la el asha
I speak with the boy and the girl in French
Behki ma'a el benet we el walad bel faransi
There is sun outside today
Fi shames el yom barra
Is it possible to know the exact date?
Mumkin el wahid ya'arif el tarikh bezzabt?

---

*With the knowledge you've gained so far, now try to create your own sentences!
*When there is no subject in the sentence, we have to create one. For example, in the last sentence, we create *el wahid,* which means literally "the one," and the verb is conjugated as for the pronoun "he."

To exchange (*money*)	Ysarrif
To call	Yittisil
Brother	Akh
Dad	Abi/baba
To sit	Ya'od
Together	Ma'a ba'dh/sawa
To change	Yghayyir
Of course	Bezzabet/taba'an
Welcome	Ahla w sahla
During	Khilal/bwa't
Years	Sana/sneen
Sky	Sama
Up	Fawa'
Down	Tahit
Sorry	Asif
To follow	Yilhaa'
To the	Le / a'al
Big	Kbir
New	Jdid
Never / ever	Abadan

I don't want to exchange this money at the bank
Ma biddi sarrif hay el masari bel bank
I want to call my brother and my son today
Biddi ittisel b akhi w ibni el yom
Of course I can come to the theater, and I want to sit together with you and with your sister
Taba'an fini iji aa'l masrah, we biddi nua'od sawa ma'ak w ma'a ikhak
I need to go down to see your new house
Lazim inzil tahit la shouf beytak eljdid
I can see the sky from the window
Fini shouf el sama mn el shibbak
I am sorry, but he wants to follow her to the store
Ana assif, bas biddu yelha'aa a'al mahal
I don't ever want to see you
Ma a'ad biddi shoufak

*In Arabic, "brother" is akh, and "dad" is baba. However, "my dad" is aby, and
"my brother" is akhi. "My sister" is ikhti, and "my mother" is imi.*
In Arabic, Lada means "at" or "with".

To allow	Yismah
To believe	Ysaddi'
Morning	Sebeh
Except	Ma a'ada/ila
To promise	Yoa'id
Good night	Tsbah a'la kheyr
To recognize	Yita'rraf
People	Nas
To move (an object)	Yharrik
To move (to a place)	Yinti'il
Far	Ba'id
Different	Mekhtelif
Man	Zalame
To enter	Yudkhul
To receive	Yistilim
Pleasant	Latif
Good afternoon	Masa el kheyr
Left / right	Yasar-shmal/yamin
Him / Her	Huwa/ Hiya

I need to allow him to go with us, he is a different man now
Lazim ismahlu yrouh ma'ana, hewwe zalame mekhtilif halla'
I believe everything except this
Bsaddi' kelshi ila had/hay
I need to move the car because my sister needs to move back home
Lazim harrik el sayyarah, la'innu ikhti bidda tinti'il a'al beyt
I promise to say good night to my parents each night
Wa'id inni 'oul tesbahu a'ala kheyr la ahli kel masa
The people from Jordan are very pleasant
El nas min el ordun kteer latifin
I need to find another hotel very quickly
Lazim la'i otel tani bsera'a
They need to receive a book for work
Mehtajen yestelmu ktab mshan el sheghel
I see the sun in the morning
Bshouf el shames el sebeh
The house is on the right side of the street
El beyt a'al taraf el yamin mn el shari'

*In Arabic, the article "the" is used when referring to countries, cities, or locations. "From Jordan" / *mn el ordun.*

To wish	Yitmanna
Bad	Mo mnih , sayyi'
To Get	Yhassil
To forget	Yinsa
Everybody / Everyone	El kel
Although	Hatta iza
To feel	Yhis
Great	Kteer mnih/kteer hilo
Next (following, after)	Elli jay/jay
To like	Yheb
In front	Iddam
Next (near, close)	A'rib
Behind	Wara
Well	Mnih / lhashi
Goodbye	Salam
Restaurant	Mat'am
Bathroom	Hammam

I don't want to wish you anything bad
Ma biddi itmannalak ay shi sayyi'
I must forget everybody from my past in order to feel relaxed
Lazim insa el kel belmadhi mshan his mertah
I am next to the person behind you
Ana janb el shakhs elli warak
There is a great person in front of me
Fi shaks kteer mnih iddami
Goodbye my friends
Salam shabab
Where is the bathroom in the restaurant?
Weyn el hammam bel mat'am
She has to buy a car before the next year
Lazim "Heyye" tishtiri sayyarah a'bil el sene el jayye
I like the house, but it is very small
Habet el beyt, bas kteer sghir
"here we used the past form for "like"

*In Syrian Arabic, "well" has two definitions, *mnih* and *lhashi*. *Mnih* is used to signify "good," while *lhashi* is used to signify "then."

101

To remove / to take out	Yikhallas min/Yshil
Please	Raja'an/ba'd iznak
Beautiful	(M)hilo, (F)hilwe
To lift	Yirfa'
Include / Including	Yishmal/ma'a
Belong	Melk
To hold	Yimsik
To check	Yitha'a'
Small	Sghir
Real	Ha'i'i
Weather	Jaw
Size	Ma'as/Hajim
High	Irtifa'
Doesn't	Ma
So (as in then)	Lhashi
So (as in very)	Kteer
Price	Si'ir
Diamond	Mas

She wants to remove this door please
Ba'd iznak, bidda tshil had el bab
This week the weather was very beautiful
Had el isbou' kan el jaw kteer helo
I need to know which is the real diamond
Lazim a'arif ay masa Heyye el ha'i'ye
We need to check the size of the house
Lazim nitha'a' min hajim el beyt
I want to lift this, so you need to raise it high
Biddi irfa' had/hay, lhalshi lazim tirfa'a a'ali
I can pay this even though that the price is so expensive
Fini idfa'a hatta law elsi'ir ghali kteer
Including everything, is this price correct?
Shamil kel shi, had elsi'ir sahih?
I want to go to sleep now because i need to wake up early and to take a taxi to the airport
Biddi rouh nam halla' la'innu lazim fii' bakkir mshan akhud taxi la elmatar

BUILDING BRIDGES

In Building Bridges, we take six conjugated verbs that have been selected after studies I have conducted for several months in order to determine which verbs are most commonly conjugated into first person. For example, once you know how to say, "I need," "I want," "I can," and "I like," you will be able to connect words and say almost anything you want more correctly and understandably. The following three pages contain these six conjugated verbs in first, second, third, fourth, and fifth person, as well as some sample sentences. Please master the entire program up until here prior to venturing onto this section.

I want	Biddi
I need	Ana lazim / ahtaj
I can	Fini / ya'dir
I like	Bheb
I go	Brouh
I have	Andi
I must / I have to	Lazim

I want to go to my house
Biddi rouh a'al beyt
I can go with you to the bus station
Fini rouh ma'ak la mahatet el bass
I need to walk to the museum
Lazim imshi la el muthaf
I like to ride the train
Bheb irkab el a'itar
I have to speak to my teacher
Lazim ihki ma'a istazi
I have a book
Andi ktab

Please master *every* single page up until here prior to attempting the following two pages!

You want / do you want? – Inte biddak/ Biddak?
He wants / does he want? - Hewwe biddu/ biddu?
She wants / does she want? – Hiyye bidda/ bidda?
We want / do we want? – Nehne bidna/ bidna?
They want / do they want? – Henne biddoun/biddoun?
You (plural) want -Intu bidkun/ bidkun?

You need / do you need? – Ana Lazim …./ ana mehtaj / lazim……?
He needs / does he need? – Hewwe lazim /hewwe mehtaj/ hewwe mehtaj?
She needs / does she need? – Hiyye lazim/hiyye mehtaja/ hiyye mehtaja?
We need / do we need? – Nehne lazimna/nehne mehtajin/ mehtajin nehne….?
They need / do they need? – Henne lazmun/henne mehtajin/lazmun?
You (plural) need? – Intu lazimkun/intu mehtajin/ intu lazimkun?

You can / can you? – Ana fini/ana be'der/fini?
He can / can he? – Hewwe fiyuu/fiyyu?
She can / can she? - Hiyye fiyya/fiyya?
We can / can we? - Nahnu fina/ fina?
They can / can they? - Henne fiyyun/ fiyyun?
You (plural) can? - Intu fikun/fikun?

You like / do you like? - Inte betheb/betheb?
He likes / does he like? - Hewwe beyheb/ beyheb?
She like / does she like? - Hiyye betheb/ betheb?
We like / do we like? – Nehne benheb(menheb)/ benheb(menheb)?
They like / do they like? - Henne beyhebbu/beyhebbu?
You (plural) like - Intu bet-hebbu/bet-hibbu?

You go / do you go? - Inte betrouh/ Betrouh inte?
He goes / does he go? - Huwwe beyrouh/ Beyrouh huwwa?
She goes / does she go? - Hiyye betrouh/ Betrouh hiyye?
We go / do we go? - Ihna benrouh/ Benrouh ihna?
They go / do they go? - Henne beyrouhu/ beyrouhu?
You (plural) go - Intu betrouhu/betrouhu?

You have / do you have? - Inte Andak/Andak?
He has / does he have? - Hewwe Andu/ hal Andu?
She has / does she have? - Hiyye Anda/ Anda?
We have / do we have? - Nehne Andna/ Andna?
They have / do they have? - Henne Andun/ Andhun?
You (plural) have - Intu Andkun/Andkun?

You must /must you? – Lazim …..../ lazim…?
He must/ must he? – Lazim ...../ lazim …..?
She must/ must she – Lazim ...../ lazim …..?
We must/ must we? – Lazim ...../ lazim …..
They must / must they? - Lazim ...../ lazim …..?
You (plural) must - Lazim ...../ lazim …..?

Please master *every* single page up until here prior to attempting the following pages!

Do you want to go?
Biddak trouh ?

Does he want to fly?
Biddu ytir?

We want to swim
Bidna nesbah

Do they want to run?
Biddun yrkdhu?

Do you need to clean?
Lazim tnadhdhif?

She needs to sing a song
Lazim tghanni ghinniye

We need to travel
Lazim nsafer

They don't need to fight
Ma lazim yetkhana'u

You (plural) need to see
Lazim tshoufu

Can you hear me?
Fik tesma'ni?

Yes, he can dance very well
Eyh, fiyyu yera'us kteer mnih

We can go out tonight
Fina nitla' el masa

They can break the wood
Fiyyun ykassru el khashab

Do you like to eat here?
Betheb takul hon?

He likes to spend time here
Beyheb ye'dhi wa'it hon

We like to fix the house
Menheb nrattib el beyt

They like to cook
Beyhebbu yutbkhu

You (plural) like my house
Bethebu beyti

Do you go to school today?
Rah trouh a'al madrasa el yom

He goes fishing
Beyrouh ysid

We are going to relax
Rayhin nrayyeh

They go to watch a film
Rayhin henne yshoufu felem

Do you have money?
Andak msari

She must look outside
Lazin hiyye ttalea' barra

We have to sign our names
Lazin nsajjil asma'na

They have to send the letter
Lazim yeba'atu el resala

You (plural) have to order
Lazim titlbou

Countries of the Middle East
Dual al-sharq al-aa'ou'satt

Lebanon	Lebnan
Syria	Sourya
Jordan	Al-urdun
Israel/Palestine/West Bank	Isra'il/Falastin/Al-diffah al-gharbiyyah
Iraq	Al-Iraq
Saudi Arabia	Il-Su'udiyyah
Kuwait	Al-kwait
Qatar	Qatar
Bahrain	Al-Bahrain
United Arab Emirates	Al-Imarat
Oman	Uman
Yemen	Al-Yaman
Egypt	Masr
Libya	Libya
Tunisia	Tunis
Algeria	Al-Jaza'ir
Morocco	Al-Maghrib

Months

January	Kanun il-thani
February	Shbat
March	Azar
April	Nisan
May	Ayyar
June	Hziran
July	Tammuz
August	Ab
September	Aylul
October	Tishrin il-Awwal
November	Tishrin ittani
December	Kanun Il-Awwal

Days of the Week

Sunday	Al-Ahad
Monday	Al-taneyn
Tuesday	Al-talata
Wednesday	Al-Arba'a
Thursday	Al-Khamis
Friday	Al-Jema'a
Saturday	Al-Sabt

Seasons

Spring	Al-Rabi'i
Summer	Al-Saif
Autumn	Al-Kharif
Winter	Al-shitey

Cardinal Directions

North	Shmal
South	Junub
East	Sharqa'
West	Gharb

Colors

Black	(M)Aswad (F)Sawda
White	(M)Abyad (F)Baida
Gray	(M)Ramadi (F)Ramadiyya
Red	(M)Ahmar (F)Hamra
Blue	(M)Azra' (F)Zara'a
Yellow	(M)Asfar (F)Safra
Green	(M)Akhdar (F)Khadra
Orange	(M)Berd'ani (F)Berda'aniyye
Purple	Lailaki
Brown	(M)Binni (F)Binniyye

Numbers

One	Wahad
Two	tneyn
Three	Tlate
Four	Arba'a
Five	Khamsa
Six	Sitte
Seven	Sab'a
Eight	Tmane
Nine	Tis'a
Ten	Ashara

Twenty	Ishrin
Thirty	Tlatin
Forty	Arb'in
Fifty	Khamsin
Sixty	Sittin
Seventy	Sab'in
Eighty	Tmanin
Ninety	Tis'in
Hundred	Miyye
Thousand	Alif
Million	Malyun

Further Grammar Exercise

*Conjugating verbs in the Damascus dialect is different from standard Arabic. There are three tenses in the Arabic language as well as the accents for the present, past, and future: The present: in this program every verb begins with *"Y,"* for example, *yktob,* "to write." What we do is delete the *"y"* letter to get the stem of the verb *ktob,* and we add a prefix, suffix, or both to each pronoun:

"I write" / *Ana bktob = b +* stem
"You write (M)" / Inte btktob = *bt +* stem
"You write (F)" / *Inti btktbi = bt +* Stem *+ i .* (The o vowel in the stem was dropped.)
"He writes" / *Hewwe byoktob = byo +* stem
"She writes" / *Heyye btoktob = bto +* stem
"They write" / *Henne byektbu = bye +* stem *+ u.* (The o vowel in the stem was dropped.)
"We write" / *Nehne bnuktob/mnuktob = bnu +* stem / *mnu +* stem
"You write (plural)" / *Into btektbu = bte +* stem *+ u.* (The o vowel in the stem was dropped.)
The prefixes of the pronouns "he" and "she" are changeable; the change is in the vowel: *byo / bto* into *bye / bte.* They change depending on the harmony of the verb, for example:
"To play" / *Yla'aab:*
"He plays" / *Hewwe byela'aab*
"She plays" / *Heyye btela'aab*
And the dropping of the vowels in the stem doesn't occur so often.

Conversational
Arabic
Quick and Easy

YATIR NITZANY

JORDANIAN ARABIC

The official language of the Hashemite Kingdom of Jordan is MSA (Modern Standard Arabic). In Jordan, MSA is taught in schools and used in newspapers and formal TV programs. However, the everyday spoken language is the Jordanian dialect, which isn't considered an official language but, rather, is a colloquial. Jordanian Arabic is considered a Levantine dialect. The Levant (al-Sham) is the region of the northwestern Middle East that includes Jordan, Syria, Israel, the West Bank, Lebanon, and Turkey's Hatay Province. Jordanian Arabic encompasses three slightly different dialects—urban, rural, and Bedouin. The colloquial of this book is the urban dialect, the Arabic that is spoken in Amman. The Jordanian dialect was influenced by many factors such as MSA, the kingdom's Bedouin community, and the Palestinian inhabitants who settled in Jordan following their displacement during the 1948 and 1967 Arab-Israeli Wars.

Spoken in: Jordan

MEMORIZATION MADE EASY

There is no doubt the three hundred and fifty words in my program are the required essentials in order to engage in quick and easy basic conversation in any foreign language. However, some people may experience difficulty in the memorization. For this reason, I created Memorization Made Easy. This memorization technique will make this program so simple and fun that it's unbelievable! I have spread the words over the following twenty pages. Each page contains a vocabulary table of ten to fifteen words. Below every vocabulary box, sentences are composed from the words on the page that you have just studied. This aids greatly in memorization. Once you succeed in memorizing the first page, then proceed to the second page. Upon completion of the second page, go back to the first and review. Then proceed to the third page. After memorizing the third, go back to the first and second and repeat. And so on. As you continue, begin to combine words and create your own sentences in your head. Every time you proceed to the following page, you will notice words from the previous pages will be present in those simple sentences as well, because repetition is one of the most crucial aspects in learning any foreign language. Upon completion of your twenty pages, *congratulations*, you have absorbed the required words and gained a basic, quick-and-easy proficiency and you should now be able to create your own sentences and say anything you wish in the Jordanian Arabic Dialect. This is a crash course in conversational Arabic, and it works!

ARABIC PRONUNCIATIONS

PLEASE MASTER THE FOLLOWING PAGE IN ARABIC PRONUNCIATIONS PRIOR TO STARTING THE PROGRAM

Kha. For Middle Eastern languages including Arabic, Hebrew, Farsi, Pashto, Urdu, Hindi, etc., and also German, to properly pronounce the kh or ch is essential, for example, *Khaled* (a Muslim name) or *Chanukah* (a Jewish holiday) or *Nacht* ("night" in German). The best way to describe kh or ch is to say "ka" or "ha" while at the same time putting your tongue at the back of your throat and blowing air. It's pronounced similarly to the sound that you make when clearing your throat. Please remember this whenever you come across any word containing a *kh* in this program.

Ghayin. The Arabic *gh* is equivalent to the "g" in English, but its pronunciation more closely resembles the French "r," rather than "g." Pronounce it at the back of your throat. The sound is equivalent to what you would make when gargling water. Gha is pronounced more as "rha," rather than as "ga." *Ghada* is pronounced as "rhada." In this program, the symbol for *ghayin* is *gh*, so keep your eyes peeled.

Aayin is pronounced as a'a, pronounced deep at the back of your throat. Rather similar to the sound one would make when gagging. In the program, the symbol for *aayin* is *a'a, u'u, o'o,* or *i'i*.

Ha is pronounced as "*ha*." Pronunciation takes place deep at the back of your throat, and for correct pronunciation, one must constrict the back of the throat and exhale air while simultaneously saying "ha." In the program, this strong h ("*ha*") is emphasized whenever *ha, ah, hi, he,* or *hu* is encountered.

NOTE TO THE READER

The purpose of this book is merely to enable you to communicate in the Jordanian Dialect. In the program itself (pages 17-39) you may notice that the composition of some of those sentences might sound rather clumsy. This is intentional. These sentences were formulated in a specific way to serve two purposes: to facilitate the easy memorization of the vocabulary and to teach you how to combine the words in order to form your own sentences for quick and easy communication, rather than making complete literal sense in the English language. So keep in mind that this is not a phrase book!

As the title suggests, the sole purpose of this program is for conversational use only. It is based on the mirror translation technique. These sentences, as well as the translations are not incorrect, just a little clumsy. Latin languages, Semitic languages, and Anglo-Germanic languages, as well as a few others, are compatible with the mirror translation technique.

Many users say that this method surpasses any other known language learning technique that is currently out there on the market. Just stick with the program and you will achieve wonders!

Again, I wish to stress this program is by no means, shape, or form a phrase book! The sole purpose of this book is to give you a fundamental platform to enable you to connect certain words to become conversational. Please also read the "Introduction" and the "About Me" section prior to commencing the program.

In order to succeed with my method, please start on the very first page of the program and fully master one page at a time prior to proceeding to the next. Otherwise, you will overwhelm yourself and fail. Please do not skip pages, nor start from the middle of the book.

It is a myth that certain people are born with the talent to learn a language, and this book disproves that myth. With this method, anyone can learn a foreign language as long as he or she follows these explicit directions:

* Memorize the vocabulary on each page

* Follow that memorization by using a notecard to cover the words you have just memorized and test yourself.

* Then read the sentences following that are created from the vocabulary bank that you just mastered.

* Once fully memorized, give yourself the green light to proceed to the next page.

Again, if you proceed to the following page without mastering the previous, you are guaranteed to gain nothing from this book. If you follow the prescribed steps, you will realize just how effective and simplistic this method is.

THE PROGRAM

Let's Begin! "Vocabulary"
(Memorize the Vocabulary)

I	I am	Ana
With you	Ma'ak / ma'ek
With him / with her	Ma'o / ma'ha
With us	Ma'na
For you	(Masc) Elak / (Fem) Elik
Without him	Bedono/ balah
Without them	Bedonhom/ balahom
Always	Daeman
Was	Kan
This, This is	(M)Hada/(F)Hadi,hadik
Is, it's, it is	Huwwi
Sometimes	Marrat
Maybe	Yimkin, Bijooz
Are you? / is it?	(M)Inta?(F) inti?/An jad
Better	Ahsan
You, you are	(M)Int / (F)inti
He / She	Huwwi/Hiyyi
From	Min

Sentences from the vocabulary (now you can speak the sentences and connect the words)

I am with you
Ana ma'ak

This is for you
(M)Hada elak/(F) Hada elik

I am from Jordan
Ana min Il-urdun

Are you from Iraq?
Int min Il-Iraq?

Sometimes you are with us at the mall
Marrat int ma'na fil mall

I am always with her
Ana daeman ma'ha

Are you without them today?
Int bedonhom elyom?

Sometimes I am with him
Marrat ana ma'o

*In Arabic, there are gender rules. Saying "for you" to a male is *ilak,* but if you are talking to a female then its *ilik.* In spoken Arabic, which has no rules, they say *Il kitab hada ilik,* and they also say *ilkitab hada mshanak* or *ilkitab hada taba'ak.*
*In spoken Arabic words like *hal / *"are" are usually dropped, and we only say *Hiyyi aklat* (she ate)? *Huwwi Nayim* (he sleeps)?, etc., which, if written in Classical Arabic,
    d have been *Hal aklat hiyyi?* or *Hal huwi Na'im?*"

I was	Ana Kunt
To be	(M)Ykun/(F)Tkun
The	Il, el, al
Same / like *(as in similar)*	Zay, nafs/Mitl
Good	Kwayyis
Here	Hon
Very	Kteer
And	Wi/W/Ow/Iw
Between	Bain
Now	Halla, Hassa
Later / After / afterwards	Ba'din
If	Law
Yes	Aaa
To	Lal
Tomorrow	Bukra
Person	Wahad/ Shakhs
Also / too / as well	Kaman/bardu

If it was between now and later

Law kan bain halla iw ba'dain

This is good as well

Hada kwayyis kaman

To be the same person

Ykun nafs ilshakhs

Yes, you are very good

Aaa, int kteer kwayyis

I was here with them

Ana kunt hon ma'hum

You and I

Int wi ana

The same day

Nafs elyom

*In the Arabic language, adjectives follow the noun. For example, "the same day" is *nafs innahar,* "small house" *is beit zrir,* "tall person" is *shakhs tawil,* and "short person" is *shakhs aseer.*

*In this program the article "the" / *il, al* will sometimes become a prefix at the beginning of the noun. For nouns beginning with *d, n, r, s, sh, t, th,* and *z,* the *l* is omitted and replaced with the initial consonant of the following noun. "The people" / *al-shakhs* is *ishakhs,* and "the Nile" / *il-nil is inil.* It is dropped when spoken, however when written it's usually *il-shaks* or *il-nil.*

*In this program, to signify "this" and "that," we will use *hada (m.), hadi (f.)* / "this" and *hadak (m.), hadik (f.)* / "that."

Me	Ana, ni, li
Ok	Tayyib, Mashi
Even if	Hatta law
No	La
Worse	A'tal/ Aswa
Where	Wain
Everything	Kul she
Somewhere	Absar wain
What	Shoo?
Almost	Ya'ni/Taqriban
There	Honak
I go	Ana rayih

Afterwards is worse
Ba'dain hada a'tal
Even if I go now
Hatta law ruh Halla
Where is everything?
Fain kul hagah?
What? I am almost there
Shoo? Ana sort honak
Where are you?
Int wain?

Fi makan literally means *in a place.*
*In Arabic the pronoun *me* has several definitions, in relation to verbs it's *ni, li.*
Li refers to any verb that relates to action of doing something to someone or
for someone. For example t*ell me, tell (to) me / Ul li,*
Ni just means me; *love me Hibbini.*
On me is Alay, in me fiyyi, to me ili
With me ma'i, in front of me qbali, from me Minni
The same rule applies for *him* and *her*, both become suffixes; *hu* and *ha*;
Love her, hebha/ love him hibbeh / love them / love us Hibhum/ hibna
Any verb that relates to doing something to someone or for someone put *L*
Tell me Ehkili, tell him Ehkilo, tell her Ehkilha, tell them Ehkilhum, tell us Ehkilna.
Adding *you* as a suffix in Arabic is *ak* or *lak. Female ik* or *lik*
Love you, Bahibbak, Bahibbik/ tell you, Ahkilak (F)Ahkilik
*In Jordanian Arabic there are a few ways of saying *no*, depending on where it falls
in the sentence. You can say *"Ma fi faydih"* but you say, if asked something like,
"are you going?" you would answer *"Laa."* to indicate *no.*
Sort is another form of saying *almost*, but can only be used in a sentence.
*In Jordanian slang there is no equivalent for "somewhere", *absar wain* is used to
indicate an anonymous place.

House	Bait
In, at, at the,in the	Fi/fi/fil /fil
Car	Sayyarah
Already	Min zaman
Good morning	Sabah ilkhair
How are you?	Kifak?
Where are you from?	(M)Int min wain?(F)Inti min wain?
Today	Elyom
Hello	Marhaba
What is your name?	Sho Ismak?/ sho Ismik?
How old are you?	Kam omrak?
Son	Ibn
Daughter	Bint
To have	(M)Induh/(F)Indha
Doesn't / isn't	Ma / mosh
Hard	Sa'b
Still	Lissah/ba'do

She doesn't have a car, so maybe she is still at the house?
Hiyyi ma indha sayyarah, mshan haik bejoz ba'dha belbait?
I am in the car already with your son and daughter
Ana bissayarah min zaman ma' ibnak iw bintk
Good morning, how are you today?
Sabah al-khair, kifak elyom?
Hello, what is your name?
Marhaba, shoo ismak?
How old are you?
Kam omrak?
This is very hard, but it's not impossible
Hada sa'b kteer, bas mosh mustahil
Where are you from?
Int min wain?

*In Jordanian Arabic, possessive pronouns become suffixes to the noun. For example, in the translation for "your," *ak* is the masculine form and *ik* feminine form.
* "your book" / ktabak (m.), ktabik (f.)
* "your house" / baitak (m.), baitik (f.)
*In the Arabic language, as well as in other Semitic languages, the article "a" doesn't exist. "She doesn't have a car" / *hiyyi ma indha sayyarah.*
*The definition of *khalas* can also be "done" or "finished."
Mshan haik means "because of," but it is also used to indicate "so."

Thank you	Shokran
For	Ala
Anything	Ay she
That, That is	(M)Hadak/(F)Hadik
Time	Wa't
But	Bas
No/ Not	Laa/Mosh
I am not	Ana mosh
Away	B'eed
Late	Mit'akkher
Similar, like	Zay/Mitl
Another/ Other	Tani
Side	Janab, Taraf
Until	Lahad
Yesterday	Imbarih
Without us	Bedonna/ balana
Since	Min, lamma
Day	Yum
Before	Abl

Thanks for anything
Shokran ala ay she
I am not here, I am away
Ana mosh hon, ana barrah
That is a similar house
Hada elbit metlo
I am from the other side
Ana min il-jiha il tanyeh
But I was here until late yesterday
Bas ana kunt hon lahad imbarih bellil
I am not at the other house
Ana mosh filbait iltani

*In Jordanian Arabic there are 3 definitions for time:
Time, wa't refers to; era, moment period, duration of time.
Time(s), marra(t) refers to; occasion or frequency.
Time, sa'ah in reference to; hour, what time is it.
Ayyi or *Ayyu* depending on where it falls in the sentence. This is the 'Ay' in Classical Arabic, meaning "any". We stress on the Y, because this is how it is pronounced in Jordanian.
Ilwa't khalas min zaman literally means "the time already ended."

119

I say / I am saying	Ana Bahki/ ba'ul
What time is it?	Kam/Addish Issa'ah?
I want	Ana biddy
Without you	Bedonak/ balak
Everywhere /wherever	Fi kul makan/ Fi ay makan
I am going	(M) Ana rayih /(F) Ana rayhah
With	Ma'
My	Lee
Cousin	(M) Ibn ammi (or) Ibn khali [uncle from mother's side), (P) owlad ammi /owlad Khali (F)bint ammi/ bint khali, (P)banat ammi, banat khali
I need	Ana mihtaj, Ana mi'taz
Right now	Halla
Night	Lail
To see	Yshuf
Light	Daw
Outside	Barrah
Without	Bedon/bala
Happy	Mabsut/Farhan
I see / I am seeing	Ana shayif

I am saying no / I say no
Ana ba'ul la'a/ ba'ul la'a
I want to see this today
Ana biddy ashuf hada elyom
I am with you everywhere
Ana ma'ak fi kul makan
I am happy without my cousins here
Ana mabsut bedon owlad ammi hon
I need to be there at night
Ana mi'taz akun honak bil-lail
I see light outside
Ana shayif daw barrah
What time is it right now?
Issa'ah kam Halla

My,li is also a possessive pronoun. *Li* means *my*, but also becomes a suffix to a noun. For example; *cousins, owlad il'am / my cousin, Ibn ammi or ibn khali* [maternal uncle's son] or *Cup, Kaseh/ my cup, Kasti*

For second and third person masculine noun; *ibn,son. Male; ak,akum/ female; ik,ikum Your son; (M)ibnak (F)ibnik/ Your (plural) son; (M)ibinhum (F)binthum* [In Jordanian, unlike Classical Arabic, plural female is not different from plural male] *His son; Ibnu; Her son, Ibnha. Our son, Ibinnaa / (M) and (F) Their son, ibinhum.*

For second and third person we use feminine noun; *car, sayyarahh Your car, sayyartak/ Your (plural) car; sayyaritkum /His car; sayyartu, Her car, sayyarit-ha, Our car, sayyaritna / (M) and (F)Their car, sayyarithum.*

Place	Makan
Easy	Sahl
To find	Yla'i
To look for/to search	Ydawwir
Near / Close	Areeb
To wait	Yestanna
To sell	Ybi'i
To use	Yista'mil
To know	Yi'raf
To decide	Yqarrir
Between	Bain
Next to	Ganb
To	Li

This place it's easy to find
Hada Ilmakan sahl yilta'a
I want to look for this next to the car
Ana biddy adawwir ala hada ganb il-sayyarah
I am saying to wait until tomorrow
Ana ba'ul nistanna la-bukrah
This table is easy to sell
Hadi il-tawlih sahl tinba'a
I want to use this
Ana biddy asta'mil hada
I need to know where is the house
Ana mihtaj a'rif makan il-bait
I want to decide between the places
Ana biddy aqarrir bain il makanain

*Please pay close attention to the conjugation of verbs, whether they are in first person, second, or third. Unlike Anglo Germanic languages, Latin languages, or even Classical Arabic, in which the first verb is conjugated and the following is always infinitive, however in colloquial Arabic it is quite different. In Spoken Arabic, for example for first person tense, the first verb is conjugated into first person and the verb as well. For example: I *need to know where is the house* in Classical Arabic it will be *Innani bihajah (I need) ila ma'rifat (to know [to know is infinitive) makan al-manzil,* in Jordanian Arabic it will be *Ana mihtag (I need) a'raf* (the verb to know is conjugated into first person as well) *makan ilbait.* The same rules apply to second as well as third person. Keep in mind the Jordanian dialect of the Arabic language is considered a colloquial, rather than an official language.

Makan il-bait literally means the *"location/place" of the house.*

Because	Laen
To buy	Yeshtari
Life	Hayah
Them, They	Hom, Hom
Bottle	Ganeneh
Book	Ktab
Mine	Eli
To understand	Yefham
Problem / Problems	Mushkeleh/ Mushkeleh
I do / I am doing	A'mal/ ana ba'mal
Of	Min
To look	Yettala'
Myself	Nafsi
Enough	Bekaffi
Food / water	Akl / Muyy
Each/ every/ all /entire	Kul/ Kul/ kul/ kul
Hotel	Fundu'

I like this hotel because I want to look at the beach
Ana Baheb hal Fundu' laenni beddy atfarraj ala-shat
I want to buy a bottle of water
Ana biddy ashtari ganeenet muyy
I do this every day
Ana ba'mil haik kul yom
Both of them have enough food
Hummi litnain indhum akl kifayeh
That is the book, and that book is mine
Hadak hoo liktab, whadak likitab eli
I need to understand the problem
Ana mihtaj afham il mushkileh
I see the view of the city from the hotel
Ana bashoof manzar il madineh min il Fundu'
I do my homework today
Ana ba'amel wajbi il manzili elyom
My entire life/ all my life
Kul Hayati/ Kul Hayati

*Tul literally means the length of.
*Bottle of water/*ganeenet muyy* the use of "of" isn't always required in Arabic.
*Haik means "like this" or "this way."

I like	Ana bahib/ Ana Yi'gibni
There is / There are	Fi
Family / Parents	Eileh/ aboy w'ommy
Why	Laish
To say	Y'ul, yehki
Something	Eshy
To go	Yruh
Ready	Jahiz
Soon	Qariban
To work	A'mil/Asawwi
Who	Meen
Busy	Mashgul
That (conjunction)	Inno, illi
I Must	Ana lazim
Important	Muhim

I like to be at my house with my parents
Ana bahib akun fi baiti ma' aboy w'ommy
I want to know why I need to say something important
Ana biddy a'rif laish lazim a'ul eshy muhim
I am there with her
Ana honak ma'ha
I am busy, but I need to be ready soon
Ana mashghul, bas mihtaj ajhaz qariban
I like to go to work
Ana bahib aruh ashshughul
Who is there?
Min honak?
I want to know if they are here, because I want to go outside
Biddy a'rif iza kanu hon, laenny biddy atla' barra
There are seven dolls
Fi sab' al'ab
I need to know that that is a good idea
Ana mihtaj a'rif inno hadi fikrah kwayyseh

*In the last sentence, we use "that" as a conjunction *(innu / inni)* and as a demonstrative pronoun *(hada / hadi)*.
**Bisur'ah* literally means "quickly."
**Mawjud* literally means "exist," but it also means "there is" or "there are" or "present."
*In Jordanian Arabic, "to go" is *yruh,* however to go out is *atla'.*

123

How much /How many	Addesh? Kam?
To bring	Yjib
With me	Ma'i
Instead	Badal
Only	Bas
When	Lamma, mata
I can / Can I?	Ana ba'adar/ ba'adar Ana?
Or	Walla/aw
Were	Kan
Without me	Bedony
Fast	Saree'
Slow	Bateei'
Cold	Barid
Inside	Juwwa
To eat	Yokel, yakol
Hot	Sukhon
To Drive	Ysu'u

How much money do I need to bring with me?
Addesh Ana mihtaj ajib masari ma'i?
Instead of this cake, I want that cake
Badal hadi elkekeh, biddy hadik elkekeh
Only when you can
Bas lamma ti'dar
They were without me yesterday
Kanu bedony imbarih
Do I need to drive the car fast or slow?
Ana mihtaj asu'u issayarah bisur'ah walla bibut'u?
It is cold inside the library
Il jaw barid juwwa il maktabeh
Yes, I like to eat this hot for my lunch
Aaa, ana baheb akul il ghada sukhun hal'ad
I can work today
Ana ba'dar ashtaghil elyom

*"Were" / kan, but for "they were," add the suffix to the pronoun, kanu. "We were" is kunna.
*In Jordanian Arabic, il jaw means "the climate, weather, temperature, etc."
*Hal'ad literally means "this way." However, when we say, sukhn hal'ad, we are saying "this hot."
*In Jordanian Arabic, the literal translation of addesh masari is "how much money."
*In Jordanian Arabic, "money" can be either masari or floos.

To answer	Yjawib
To fly	Ytir
Time / Times	Wa't/Marrah, Aw'at/Marrat
To travel	Ysafir
To learn	Yit'allam
How	Kaif
To swim	Yisbah
To practice	Yitdarrab
To play	Yil'ab
To leave (something)	Yitrok
Many /much /a lot	Kteer
I go to	Ana rayih ala
First	Awwal
World	Alam
Around	Hawalin

I want to answer many questions
Ana biddy ajawib ala as'ilih kteereh
I must travel to Dubai today
Ana Lazim asafir ala Dubai elyom
I need to learn to swim at the pool
Ana mihtaj at'allam issibaha fi birkit il muy
I want to learn to play better tennis
Ana biddy at'allam li'b il tennis kwayyis
I want to leave this here for you when I go to travel the world
Ana biddy atrok hada hon mshanak, lamma asafir walef il-alam
Since the first time
Min awwal marrah
The children are yours
Hadul owladak

*In Jordanian Arabic, "to leave (something)" is *atrok*.
"To leave (a place)" is *atrok il makan*.
*In Jordanian Arabic there are 3 definitions for "time":
-Time, *wa't* refers to; era, moment period, duration of time.
-Time(s), *marra(t)* refers to; occasion or frequency.
-Time, *sa'ah* in reference to; hour, what time is it?
Hadul literally means "those" but again, when we want to say
"the children are yours" in Jordanian, we say *hadul owladak*,
meaning "the children in question" or "the children referred to."
*With the knowledge you've gained so far, now try to create your
own sentences!

Nobody / Anyone	Wala wahad/ay wahad
Against	Did/mosh ma'
Us	Ihna
To visit	Yzur
Mom / Mother	Mama/ummi
To give	Ya'ti
Which	Ay
To meet	Yilta'i
Someone	Wahad
Just	Mugarrad/bas
To walk	Il mashi'
Week	Usbu'u
Towards	Bittijah
Than	Min
Nothing	Wala eshi

Something is better than nothing

Eshi ahsan min wala eshi

I am against her

Ana didha / Ana mosh ma'ha

We go to visit my family each week

Ihna binzur ahli kul usbu'u

I need to give you something

Ana mihtaj a'teek hagah

Do you want to go meet someone?

Biddak truh t'abil wahad?

I was here on Wednesdays as well

Ana kunt hon al-arbi'a Kaman

Do you do this everyday?

Int bti'mal haik kul yum?

You need to walk, but not towards the house

Int mihtaj titmasha, bas mosh bittijah il-bait

*In Jordanian Arabic when using the pronoun *you* as a direct and indirect object pronoun (the person who is actually affected by the action being carried out) in relation to a verb, the pronoun, *you*, becomes a suffix to that verb. That suffix becomes *(Masc)ak (Fem)ik.* To give, *yiddi* / to give you, *yiddik* To tell, *yi'ul/* to tell you, *(M)yi'ullak (F)yi'ullik.* See you, *Ashufak* /to see you(Plural), *(M)Ashufkum, (F)Ashufkum* [in Jordanian they address males and females the same].

For third person male add *"u"* (plural)hum and for female add *"ha"* (plural)hum. *Tell him A'ullu / tell her, A'ullaha / see them, (M)Ashufhum (F)Ashufhum / see us, Shufna.*

*The definition of *I'mal kidah* is *"do this"* or *"do it like this".* The most common standalone definition of *Kidah* is *"like this".*

I have	Ana Indi
Don't	Ma
Friend	Sahib/ Sahbiti [F], Sahbi [M]
To borrow	Yetdayan/yesta'ir
To look like / resemble	Yishbah
Grandfather	Jid
To want	Biddy
To stay	Ydal
To continue	Ykammil
Way (road, path)	Tari'/share'
Way (method)	Tari'a'
I dont	Ana ma, Ana mosh
To show	Ywarji
To prepare	Yjahhiz
I am not going	Ana mosh rayeh

Do you want to look like Salim
Int Biddak tseer tisabah Salim?
I want to borrow this book for my grandfather
Ana biddy asta'ir hada halikitab lajiddi
I want to drive and to continue on this way to my house
Ana biddy asu' wa akammil ala hada il-tari' lahad-ilbaiti
This isn't the way to do this
Mish ay he ettari'a la'amal hal-she?
I have a friend there, that's why I want to stay in Amman
Ana indi sahib honak, mshan haik biddy adal fi-Amman
I am not going to see anyone here
Ana mish rah ashuf ay wahad hon
I need to show you how to prepare breakfast
Ana mihtaj awarjik kaif tjahiz liftoor
Why don't you have the book?
Laish ma indak liktab?
That is incorrect, I don't need the car today
hada mosh sahih, ana ma biddy il-sayyarah elyom

*Sahih means "correct"; however, mosh sahih means "incorrect."
*Indak means "to have." "I have" is ana indi. However, "I don't have" is Ana ma indi.
*Lahad means "up to" or "to" as the final destination. It can also mean "until."
*In Jordanian Arabic, "to want" is biddo.
* "I want" / biddy, "he wants" / biddo, "she wants" / bidha,
*Tseer means "become."
*Halikitba it is a way of saying "this book" by merging "this" with "the book" (ha-li-kitab).
' means "will," indicating future tense, ana rah / "I will."

To remember	Yitzakkar
Your	Lak
Number	Raqam
Hour	Sa'ah
Dark / darkness	'Itmeh
About / on the	'An/ alal
Grandmother	Jiddeh/ taiti
Five	Khamsa
Minute / Minutes	Di'i'ah/da'ayi'
More	Akthar
To think	Yfakker
To do	A'mil/Asawwi
To come	Yiji
To hear	Yisma'a
Last	Akhir
To talk / To Speak	Ahki/ a'ul

You need to remember my number
Int mihtaj titzakkar raqami
This is the last hour of darkness
Hadi akhir sa'a min il-'itmeh
I want to come to hear my grandmother speak Arabic
Ana biddy aji asma'a jidditi btehky Arabi
I need to think more about this, and what to do
Ana mihtaj afakker aktar behal'mawdoo', w'sho assawi
From here to there, it's only five minutes
Min hon lahonak khamis da'a'yi' bas
The school on the mountain
Il madraseh alal-jabal

Mawdoo' literally means "topic," "subject."
*In Spoken Arabic, "on" is *ala,* and "the" is *al.* If you were to write it in Arabic, *ala* ("on") and *al* ("the") are separate, but because Jordanians make them sound like one word when they utter them, the *ala* and *al* are joined, and it becomes *alal.*

Early	Bakkeer
To leave (to go)	Yutruk
Again	Marah tanyiih
Arabic	Arabi
To take	Yakhud
To try	Yjarrib
To rent	Yesta'jir
Without her	Bedonha
We are	Ihna
To turn off	Yitfi
To ask	Yes'al
To stop	Ywa'if
Permission	Izn
While	Fatra

He needs to leave and rent a house at the beach
Huwwi mihtaj yutruk wi yista'jir bait ala al bahir
I want to take the test without her
Ana biddy akhod il'imtihan bedonha
We are here a long while
Ihna rah ndal hon lafatrah tawileh
I need to turn off the lights early tonight
Ana mihtaj atfi iddaw bakkeer illailih
We want to stop here
Ihna bedna nwa'if hon
We are from Amman
Ihna min amman
The same building
Nafs Il-binayeh
I want to ask permission to leave
Ana biddy atlub izn ashan atruk

*In Jordanian Arabic, *rah ndal* gives the meaning that we have been and will continue to be here for a long while. *Rah ndal,* literally speaking, means "will stay."
*In Jordanian Arabic, *mshan* means "because," but also here in Jordanian usage, it simply means "to" and "in order to."

To open	Yeftah
A bit, a little, a little bit	Shway
To pay	Yedfa'a
Once again	Kaman Marrah/marrah tanyeh
There isn't/ there aren't	Ma fi
Sister	Ukht
To hope	Yetmanna
To live (to exist)	Y'ish
To live (in a place)	Yuskun
Nice to meet you	Fursah sa'ideh
Name	Ism
Last name	Ism il ailih
To return	Raj'ah
Syria	Surya
Door	Bab/bawwabah

I need to open the door for my sister
Ana mihtaj aftah il-bab la ukhti
I need to buy something
Ana Mihtaj ashtari eshi
I want to meet your sisters
Biddy alta'ai bekhawatak
Nice to meet you, what is your name and your last name
Fursah sa'idih, sho ismak w'ismi a'iltak?
To hope for a little better
Yitmanna eshi ahsan shway
I want to return to Qatar
Ana biddy Arja'a ala Qatar
I want to live 100 years
Ana biddy a'ish mit saneh
I need to return your book
Ana mihtaj arajji'lak li-ktab
Why are you sad right now?
(M)Int laish za'alan halla'? (F) Inti laish za'alaneh halla?
There aren't any people here
Ma fi wala wahad hon
There isn't enough time to go to Syria today
Ma fi wa't kifayeh larroha ala surya elyom

To happen	Yseer
To order	Yutlub/yu'mur
To drink	Yishrab
Excuse me	Lau samaht/ min fadlak
Child	(M)Walad, (F)bint
Woman	Marah
To begin / To start	Yibda'/yballish
To finish	Yikhallas
To help	Ysa'id
To smoke	Ydakkhin
To love	Yhib
Afternoon	Ba'd idduhr

This must happen today
Hada lazim yseer elyom
Excuse me, my child is here with me as well
Min fadlak, ibni Kaman ma'i hon
I love you
Bahibbak
I see you
Ana shayfak
I need you at my side
Ana mihtajak janbi
I need to begin soon in order to be able to finish before 3 o'clock in the afternoon
Ana mihtaj abda' bsur'ah mshan akhallis abl issa'ah talatih ba'd idduhur
I need help
Ana mihtaj musa'dih
I don't want to smoke once again
Ana ma biddy adakkhin marrah tanyeh
I want to learn how to speak Arabic
Ana biddy at'allam kaif ahki Arabi

*"To help" is *asa'id*, however "help!" is *mus'adih*.
(I need help, I need rescue / *ana mihtaj mus'adih*).

To read	Qira'ah
To write	Kitabih
To teach	Ydarris/ y'allim
To close	Ysakkir
To choose	Yikhtar/ yna'i
To prefer	Yfaddil
To put	Yhut
Less	A'al
Sun	Shams
Month	Shahr
I Talk	Ana bahki/ ba'ul
Exact	Bizzabt/ tamam

I need this book in order to learn how to read and write in the Arabic language in order to study in Jordan
Ana mihtaj halikitab mshan at'allam il-qira'ah wilkitabih billughah il-arabiiyyeh mshan adrus fil'ordon
I want to close the door of the house
Ana biddy asakkir bab il-bait
I prefer to put the gift here
Ana bafaddil ahutt il-hadiyyih hon
I want to pay less than you for the dinner
Ana biddy adfa' a'al minnak lal'asha
I speak with the boy and the girl in French
Ana bahki ma'a ilwalad wil-bint bil faransi
There is sun outside today
Il-shams barrah tal'ah elyom
Is it possible to know the exact date?
Mumkin ni'raf il-tarikh bizzabt?
I want to sleep
Biddy nam
Where is the airport
Wain il-matar

To exchange (*money*)	Sarf/tabdil 'omlih
To call	yittasil
Brother	Akhu
Dad	Baba/ ab
To sit	A'ud
Together	Ma' ba'd/ sawa
To change	Yghayyir/yitghayyar
Of course/certainly	Tab'an/Akeed
Welcome	Ahlin
During	Ayyam, Wa'it
Years	Sneen/ sanawat
Sky	Sama
Up	Fu'
Down	Taht
Sorry	Asif
To follow	Yilha'
To the	Lal
Big	Kbeer
New	Jdeed
Never / ever	Abadan/ niha'yyan

I don't want to exchange this money at the bank
Ana ma biddy abaddil il-'omlch fil bank
I want to call my brother and my son today
Ana biddy attasil bi akhuy wibni elyom
Of course I can come to the theater, and I want to sit together with you and with your sister
Akid rah a'dar aji al-masrah, wbiddy aa'ud ma'ak wima'a ukhtak
I need to go down to see your new house
Ana mihtaj anzil mshan ashuf baitak li-jdeed
I can see the sky from the window
Ana ba'dar ashuf issama min il-shubbak
I am sorry, but he wants to follow her to the store
Ana assif, bas huwwi biddo yilha'ha ala-l-mahal
I never want to see you
Ana ma biddy ashufak Abadan

*In Jordanian Arabic, "brother" is *akh*, and "dad" is *baba*. However, "my dad" is *aboy*, and "my brother" is *akhuy*. "My sister" is *ukhti*, and "my mother" is *ommi*.
*In the English language the verb "to go down" isn't commonly used. However, in many foreign languages, the use of this verb is quite prevalent.
*This *isn't* a phrase book! The purpose of this book is *solely* to provide you with the tools to create *your own* sentences!

To allow	Yismah
To believe	Yisadda'/yi'min
Morning	Sabah
Except	Illa
To promise	Yew'id
Good night	Tisbah ala khair
To recognize	Yit'arraf
People	Ahl, nas, bani admin
To move (an object)	Yharrik
To move (to a place)	Yinta'il
Far	B'eed
Different	Gher
Man	Zalameh
To enter	Yfoot/yidkhul
To receive	Yistalim
Pleasant	Latif/ Zarif/ habboob
Good afternoon	Masa'a-il-Khair
Left / right	Shmal/ yasar, Yameen
Him / Her	Lu/ lha

I need to allow him to go with us, he is a different man now
Ana mihtaj asmahlu yiji ma'na, la'ennu tghayyar halla w-sar zalameh gher
I believe everything except this
Ana basaddi' kul she illa hal-she
I need to move the car because my sister needs to return home
Ana mihtaj aharrik il-sayyarah laenno ukhti mihtajeh tirga'a al-bait
The people from Jordan are very pleasant
Il-urduniyyin zarifeen kteer
I need to find another hotel very quickly
Ana mihtaj ala'i fundu' tani bsur'ah kteer
They need to receive a book for work
Hummi mihtajin yistilmu ktab la-shughul
I see the sun in the morning
Ana bashuf ilshams il-subuh
The house is on the other end of the street
Il-bait mawjud ala ilnahyeh iltanyeh min il-shari'

*In Arabic, the article "the" is used when referring to countries, cities, or locations. "From Jordan" / *min il urdun.*
**W-sar* means "and became."

To wish	Yitmanna
Bad	Sayyi', 'atil
To Get	Yjib/ yakhud
To forget	Yinsa
Although	Ma' innu/ raghim
Everybody / Everyone	Kul wahad/ il-kul
To feel	Yhis
Past	Zaman
Next (following, after)	Illy-ba'du/ ilmarrah-ijjay
To like	Yi'jib/ yhib
In front	Iddam
Next (near, close)	Areeb / janb
Behind	Wara
Well (as in doing well)	Kwayyis
Goodbye	Ma' issalamah
Restaurant	Mat'am
Bathroom	Hammam

I don't want to wish you anything bad

Ana ma biddy atmannalak ayya she 'atil

I must forget everybody from my past in order to feel well

Ana lazim ansa kul illi kanu fi hayati zaman mshan aseer kwayyis

I am next to the person behind you

Ana janb ilshakhs illi warak

There is a person in front of me

Fi shakhs iddami

Goodbye my friends

Ma' issalamih ya s-habi

Where is the bathroom in the restaurant?

Wain Il-hamman illi fil-mat'am?

She has to buy a car before the next year

Hiyyi lazim tishtari sayyarah abl il-sanih ijjay

I like the house, but it is very small

Il-bait ajibni, bas huwwi sgheer kteer

*In Jordanian Arabic, *baseer* means "to be" or "to become."

Illi means "that."

To remove / to take out	Yishil
Please	Min fadlak/ law samaht
Beautiful	(M)Helo, (F) helweh
To lift	Yirfa'a
Correct	Mazbut
Belong	Taba'
To hold	Yimsik, yitmassak
To check	Yifhas
Small	Sgheer
Real	Ha'i'i
Weather	Ijjaw/ il-ta's
Size	Hajm/ 'yas/ kubr/ masahah
High	'Ali
Doesn't	Ma
So (as in then)	Mshan hek/ ya'ni
So (as in very)	Jiddan, kteer
Price	Si'r/ ha'
Diamond	Almas

She wants to remove this door please
Hiyyi bidha tshil hal-bab min fadlak
This week the weather was very beautiful
Il-usbu'u hada, il gau kan gamil kteer
I need to know which is the real diamond
Ana mihtaj a'araf ayya wahdeh fihum hiyyi il al-massih il-ha'i'iyyih
We need to know the size of the house
Ihna mihtajin ni'rif kubr il-bait
I want to lift this, so you need to hold it high
Ana biddy arfa'a hada, ashan haik int mihtaj timiskuh 'ali
I can pay this even though that the price is so expensive
Ana mumkin adfa'a hal-mablagh ma' innuh ghali kteer
Is this price correct?
Hassi'ir bekon mazbut?

*In Jordanian Arabic, *il-mablagh* means "the amount."
*In Arabic, the articles "this" and "that" become reversed when preceding a noun. "This" (*da*) "week" (*usbu'u*) becomes *hada il-'usbu'u.*
Hasbaana means "bill

136

BUILDING BRIDGES

In Building Bridges, we take six conjugated verbs that have been selected after studies I have conducted for several months in order to determine which verbs are most commonly conjugated into first person. For example, once you know how to say, "I need," "I want," "I can," and "I like," you will be able to connect words and say almost anything you want more correctly and understandably. The following three pages contain these six conjugated verbs in first, second, third, fourth, and fifth person, as well as some sample sentences. Please master the entire program up until here prior to venturing onto this section.

I want	Ana biddy
I need	Ana mihtaj
I can	Ana ba'dar, ana mumkin
I like	Ana bi'jibni, ana bahib
I go	Ana aruh
I have	Ana indi
I must / I have to	Ana lazim, wajib alay

I want to go to my house

Ana biddy aruh ala baiti

I can go with you to the bus station

Ana mumkin aruh ma'ak ala mujamma' il-basat

I need to walk to the museum

Ana mihtaj amshi lal mat-haf

I like to ride the train

Ana bahib arkab il-qitar

I have to speak to my teacher

Ana lazim ahki ma' il-mudarris taba'i

I have a book

Ana indi ktab

Please master pages #81-#137, prior to attempting the following pages!!

You want / do you want - Int biddak/ Int biddak?
He wants / does he want - Huwwi biddo/ huwwi biddo?
She wants / does she want - Hiyyi bidha/ Hiyyi bidha?
We want / do we want - Ihna bidna/ Ihna bdna?
They want / do they want - Hummi bidhom/ Hummi bidhom?
You (plural) want / - Intu bidko/ Intu bidko?

You need / do you need - Int mihtaj/ int mihtaj?
He needs / does he need – Huwwi mihtaj/ huwwi mihtaj?
She needs / does she need - Hiyyi mihtajah/ Hiyyi mihtajah?
We need / do we need - Ihna mihtajin/ ihna mihtajin?
They need / do they need - Hummi mihtajin/ Hummi mihtajin?
You (plural) need/ do you need? - Intu mihtajin/ intu Mihtajin?

You can / can you - Int bti'dar/ Int bti'dar?
He can / can he - Huwwi byi'dar/ Huwwi byi'dar?
She can / can she - Hiyyi bti'dar/ Hiyyi bti'dar?
We can / can we - Ihna bni'dar/ Ihna bni'dar?
They can / can they - Hummi byi'daru/ Hummi byi'daru?
You (plural) can - Intu bti'daru/ Intu bti'daru?

You like / do you like – Int byi'ijbak/ Int byi'ijbak?
He likes / does he like – Huwwi yi'ijbuh/ Huwwi yi'ijbuh?
She like / does she like – Hiyyi yi'jibha/ Hiyyi yi'jibha?
We like / do we like – Ihna byi'jibna/ Ihna byi'jibna?
They like / do they like - Hummi byi'jibhum/ Hummi byi'jibhum?
You (plural) like – Intu byi'jibkum/ Intu byi'jibkum?

You go / do you go - Int bitruh/ int bitruh?
He goes / does he go - Huwwi biyruh/ huwwi Biyruh?
She goes / does she go - Hiyyi bitruh/ hiyyi Bitruh?
We go / do we go - Ihna binruh/ ihna binruh?
They go / do they go – Hummi biyruhu/ Hummi biyruhu?
You (plural) go/ do you go – Intu bitruhu/ Intu bitruhu?

You have / do you have – Int indak/ Int indak?
He has / does he have – Huwwi induh/ Huwwi induh?
She has / does she have – Hiyyi indha/ Hiyyi indha?
We have / do we have – Ihna indna/ Ihna indna?
They have / do they have – Hummi indhum/ Hummi indhum?
You (plural) have/ do you have – Intu indku/ Intu indku?

You must /must you? – Int lazim/ Int lazim?
He must/ must he? – Huwwi lazim/ Huwwi lazim?
She must/ must she –Hiyyi lazim/ Hiyyi lazim?
We must/ must we? - Ihna lazim/ Ihna lazim?
They must / must they? – Hummi lazim/ Hummi lazim?
You (plural) must/ must you? – Intu lazim/ Intu lazim?

138

Do you want to go?
Int biddak truh?
Does he want to fly?
Huwwi biddo ytir?
We want to swim
Ihna bidna nisbah
Do they want to run?
Hummi bidhom yurukdu?
Do you need to clean?
Int mihtaj tnaddif?
She needs to sing a song
Hiyyi mihtajih tghanni ughniyih
We need to travel
Ihna mihtajin nsafir
They don't need to fight
Hummi mish mihtajin yitkhana'u
You (plural) need to see
Intu mihtajin tshufu
Can you hear me?
Int bti'dar tisma'ni?
Yes, he can dance very well
Aaa, huwwi byi'dar yur'us kteer kwayyis
We can go out tonight
Ihna mumkin nitla' il-lailih
They can break the wood
Hummi byi'daru ykasru il-khashab
Do you like to eat here?
Int Bithib takul hon?

He likes to spend time here
Huwi bihib ymaddi alwa't hon
We like to fix the house
Ihna binhib nzabbit il-bait
They like to cook
Hummi bihibbu al-tabikh
You (plural) like my house
Intu 'ajabku baiti
Do you go to school today?
Int rayih al-madrasih elyom?
He goes fishing
Huwi rayih yseed samak
We are going to relax
Rah nastarkhi
They go to watch a film
Hummi rayhin yihdaru film
Do you have money?
Int indak masari?
She must look outside
Hiyyi Lazim tittala' barra
We have to sign our names
Ihna lazim nwaqqi' taht asamina
They have to send the letter
Hummi lazim ywaddo il-risalih
You (plural) have to order
Antu lazim tutulbu

Countries of the Middle East
Dowal il-sharq il-awsat

Lebanon	Lubnan
Syria	Surya
Jordan	Il-urdun
Israel/Palestine/West Bank	Isra'il/Falastin/il-diffih il-gharbiyyih
Iraq	Il-Ira'a
Saudi Arabia	Il-Suudiyah
Kuwait	Il-Kuwait
Qatar	Qatar
Bahrain	Il-Bahrain
United Arab Emirates	Il-Imarat
Oman	Uman
Yemen	Yaman
Egypt	Masir
Libya	Libya
Tunisia	Tunis
Algeria	Il-jaza'ir
Morocco	Il-Maghrib

Months

January	Kanun il-thani
February	Shbat
March	Athar
April	Nisan
May	Ayyar
June	Huzayran
July	Tammuz
August	Aab
September	Aylul
October	Tishreen awwal
November	Tishreen thani
December	Kanun awwal

Days of the Week

Sunday	Yum il-ahad
Monday	Yum il-ithnin
Tuesday	Yum il-thulatha'
Wednesday	Yum al-'arbi'aa
Thursday	Yum il-khamees
Friday	Yum il-jom'a
Saturday	Yum issabt

Seasons

Spring	Rabee'
Summer	Saif
Autumn	Khareef
Winter	Shita

Cardinal Directions

North	Shamal
South	Ganoob
East	Sharq
West	Gharb

Colors

Black	(M)Aswad (F)Suda
White	(M)Abyad (F)Baida
Gray	(M)Ramadi (F)Ramadiyyih
Red	(M)Ahmar (F)Hamra
Blue	(M)Azra' (F)Zar'a
Yellow	(M)Asfar (F)Safra
Green	(M)Akhdar (F)Khadra
Orange	(M)Burtuqali/(F)Burtuqaliyyih
Purple	(M)kuhli/(F)kuhliyyeh
Brown	(M)Bunni (F)Bunniyyeh

Numbers

One	Wahd
Two	Itnain
Three	Talatih
Four	Arba'ah
Five	Khamsih
Six	Sittih
Seven	Sab'ah
Eight	Tamanyih
Nine	Tis'ah
Ten	'Asharah

Twenty	'Ishreen
Thirty	Talateen
Forty	Arb'in
Fifty	Khamseen
Sixty	Sitteen
Seventy	Sab'een
Eighty	Tamaneen
Ninety	Tis'een
Hundred	Miyyih
Thousand	Alf
Million	Malyun

CONCLUSION

Congratulations! You have completed all the tools needed to master the Lebanese, Palestinian, Syrian and Jordanian Arabic Dialects, and I hope that this has been a valuable learning experience. Now you have sufficient communication skills to be confident enough to embark on a visit to an Arab speaking country, impress your friends, and boost your resume so good luck.

This program is available in other languages as well, and it is my fervent hope that my language learning programs will be used for good, enabling people from all corners of the globe and from all cultures and religions to be able to communicate harmoniously. After memorizing the required three hundred and fifty words, please perform a daily five-minute exercise by creating sentences in your head using these words. This simple exercise will help you grasp conversational communications even more effectively. Also, once you memorize the vocabulary on each page, follow it by using a notecard to cover the words you have just memorized and test yourself and follow that by going back and using this same notecard technique on the pages you studied during the previous days. This repetition technique will assist you in mastering these words in order to provide you with the tools to create your own sentences.

Every day, use this notecard technique on the words that you have just studied.

Everything in life has a catch. The catch here is just consistency. If you just open the book, and after the first few pages of studying the program, you put it down, then you will not gain anything. However, if you consistently dedicate a half hour daily to studying, as well as reviewing what you have learned from previous days, then you will quickly realize why this method is the most effective technique ever created to become conversational in a foreign language. My technique works! For anyone who doubts this technique, all I can say is that it has worked for me and hundreds of others.

NOTE FROM THE AUTHOR

Thank you for your interest in my work. I encourage you to share your overall experience of this book by posting a review. Your review can make a difference! Please feel free to describe how you benefited from my method or provide creative feedback on how I can improve this program. I am constantly seeking ways to enhance the quality of this product, based on personal testimonials and suggestions from individuals like you.
Thanks and best of luck,
Yatir Nitzany

Printed in Great Britain
by Amazon

40950934R00083